By Theft and Murder:

A Beginner's Guide to

the Occupation of Palestine.

Second Edition July 2003

ISBN 0-9525744-3-8

Published by Spare Change Books & Active Distribution
Spare Change Books, Box 26, 136-138 Kingsland High Street,
Hackney, London E8 7SN, UK sparechangebooks@yahoo.co.uk

Distribution:
A.K., PO BOX 40682, San Francisco, CA 94149-6082 USA
A.K., PO BOX 12766, Edinburgh EH8 9YE, Scotland
Jon Active, BM Active, London WC1N 3XX

Printed in Great Britain

Designed by Gini Simpson/ Ted Curtis

www.palsolidarity.org
www.ism-london.org

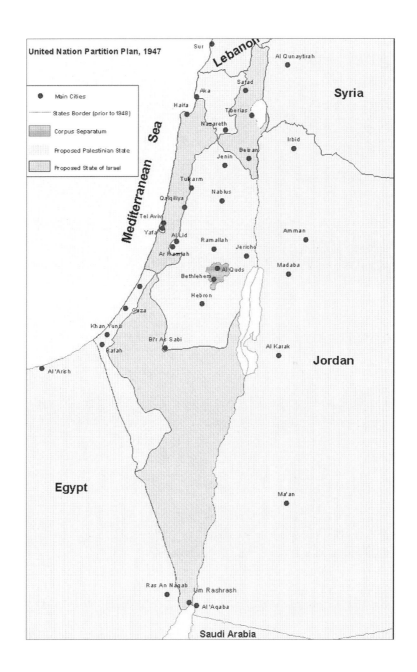

United Nation Partition Plan, 1947

Main Cities
States Border (prior to 1948)
Corpus Separatum
Proposed Palestinian State
Proposed State of Israel

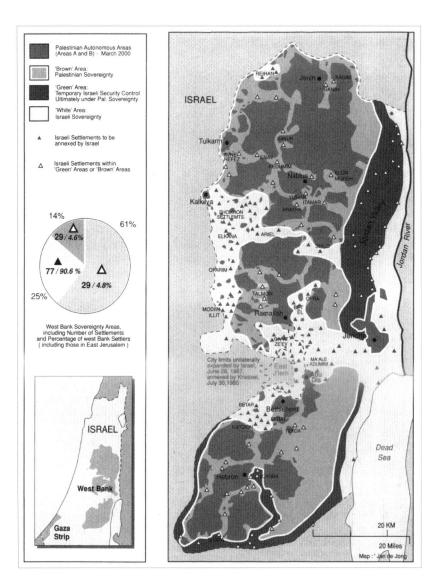

Ehud Barak's 'generous offer' made during the Oslo negotiations.

4

Contents

Acknowledgements

As good or bad as this book might be, I couldn't have written it without purloining the notes of Rachel Boyd, George Roussopoulos, and Greg Muttitt. Big thanks also to Ghassan Bannoura and Hanna Braun for their insights and information, to Huwaidaa and Adam Shapiro and Helen Barclay for the update notes, to Georgie for assistance, and to everybody else who was and is there. We are all tapdancers now. Blessings also be upon Fiona, Robert, and Dean & Alexis at AKUK.

"By theft and murder
they took the land
now everywhere the walls spring up
at their command…"

- Leon Rosselson

Introduction

I had wanted to travel to Israel/Palestine for a couple of years, following a week's visit to Rome in February of 1999. Although I am not a religious person, I'm very interested in religious history as I consider it to be the formative basis of the history of the world in which most of us have to exist. However convoluted and mythologised it may seem to be, or perhaps has become, it's all that we have; and anyway, isn't most history right up to the present day, that is available to most people, also to be taken with a large pinch of salt?

However, due primarily to the representation of "the region" in the mass media, I kept putting it off and putting it off. To watch the news reports, a reasonable person might conclude that this part of the world was the last outpost of Old Testament barbarism, populated almost entirely by religious zealots and other maniacs who were desperate to propel themselves into the afterlife at the first opportunity. To put it quite simply, I was more than a little wary of going there alone, and nobody seemed to want to accompany me for some reason. I once offered a close friend, ordinarily a very adventurous soul, £200 toward his costs; but still he declined.

Although I had read a little radicalised history of the 'Arab-Israeli conflict', most of this seemed to be very much a political overview, and I wanted to see what life was really like for people on the ground there. Travel guides that normally seemed to be quite progressive and left-of-centre drew back in the case of Israel/Palestine, not wanting to say anything that might affect their sales figures. The Lonely Planet guide[i], for example, details the history of the land of Palestine as merely being the history of the state of Israel, beginning its attentions with a brief biography of Theodor Hertzl[ii] in the late nineteenth century, and then suddenly jumping forward to 1948.

Then the second Intifada came along, jump-started as it was by Ariel Sharon's mob-handed, calculated, and Ehud Barak[iii]-sponsored visit to the Al-Aqsa mosque in east Jerusalem in September 2001. Now most of the ancient shrines and sites that I had wanted to see at first hand – almost all of which seemed to be situated in the West Bank[iv] – were becoming more and more inaccessible to me. Every night I watched on BBC News 24 as more and more military blockades and razor wire went up all along the green line[v], and Merkava tanks rolled relentlessly into seemingly defenceless Palestinian villages that had only a fledgling police force to protect them. Still entranced, I kept on reading my Chomsky and Edward Said, becoming more and more enraged about what was going on there, yet at the same time feeling absolutely powerless to affect it in any way. What could I do? I could speak neither Hebrew nor Arabic, and I wouldn't even be allowed into the places that were really suffering.

I had read George Monbiot's piece in the Guardian[vi] on the Women in Black, curiously entitled "Hell's Grannies", and was wondering on and off how they had managed to get out to the West Bank. Then, in October of last year, I came across a flyer at the anarchist bookfair in London. 'Go to Palestine now!' it exhorted me, 'Palestine needs you. As internationals we can make a real difference to the suffering of the Palestinian people'. Or something like that. So I went. And what I found there was not the crass mass-media image of Kalashnikov-toting Islamic fundamentalists and suicide bombers, but a gentle and yet unbelievably resilient people. A people who are forced to live under the absolutely intolerable conditions of ongoing ethnic cleansing, extreme racist apartheid, and the daily routine murders of their loved ones in their own homeland. You might expect that such brutalising conditions would give rise to a culture of extreme hatred for all things British and American[vii], yet everywhere we went we were greeted with smiling faces, warm handshakes and redolent hospitality. Whilst I recognise that the Jewish people were in dire need of a land to call their own after the 2000 years of anti-semitism and persecution that culminated in the nazi holocaust of 1933-45, in my view the buggered child adopting the cynicism and the methods of its abuser is not the best way of going about this. Furthermore, it doesn't even work. Israel has become a military garrison, locked into a cycle of tit-for-tat massacres that will ultimately destroy it. But it's not too late for hope. Now read on.

Getting There...

It would be reasonable to assume that TLV's[viii] airport security may have been expecting peace activists to come in on the afternoon flight from Britain. It was December 15th, the designated day for arrival for the ISM's[ix] fortnight of NVDA[x] in the occupied territories, and sure enough there were the requisite pair of goons waiting to pull me off to one side at the foot of the staircase as I stepped off the plane. They were very casual-looking goons, mind you: short sleeves, loafers and a security tag on a little chain around the neck. I thought that this must just be routine, and that I was unlucky to have been selected. Go with it and be patient, Teddy.

The flight had been comfortable enough: a Boeing 777, 9 seats wide, with a choice of movies and even a free pair of socks. Now, you don't get that with Ryanair. I should have known that the comfort wasn't to last. My guardian demon went straight into it. Why was I in Israel? To visit old archaeological sites, and some Christian churches. Where are these churches? They're mostly in Jerusalem. Archaeological sites from which area? Jerusalem. From which area? Jerusalem. From which ERA? Oh, sorry. Pause. Old Testament. What is your occupation? I'm a part-time student. And if you are a student, who is paying for this trip? Oh, my. My mother. It's a Christmas present.

Don't you have to be in school right now?, he went on. No, it's the Christmas break. When were you in Egypt?[xi] In June. What were you *doing* in Egypt? Visiting ancient archaeological sites. Where were you in Egypt? In the Valley of the Kings, in Luxor. Do you know people in Egypt? No, it was a cheap package holiday. Is this your first time in Israel? Yes. Do you know anyone here? No. Where will you be staying in Israel? I have a reservation at a hostel in Jaffa. Can I see the reservation please? I fumbled around in my shoulder bag and I showed him the reservation. OK. Passport again, please. All the time that he was looking at it he was attempting to flick between the pages, as if more than a little suspicious that I had tried to glue a couple of

11

them together to hide an entrance/exit visa stamp from Lebanon or Saudi Arabia or Afghanistan. How long are you staying in Israel for?, he continued. For 9 days, until the 24th of December. Can I see your return ticket please, sir? I showed him the booking reference, what they call an e-ticket. He waited a while and then he handed it back. OK sir, very sorry for the inconvenience. He waved me on, waiting for another suspicious character in a Big Country shirt to come on down the steps. I managed to just miss the transit bus to the arrivals hall. I turned to Liz, a woman whom I had met briefly at an affinity group meeting the month before at her house in Stamford Hill. "Damn!" I said. "I could have got on that bus!" She blanked me. We had agreed at our meeting not to acknowledge each other on the way into the country, so as to avoid being seen as travelling in a group, and thus drawing unnecessary attention to ourselves. I was on my own for now.

*****

"Why are you coming to Israel?" asked the woman in the passport-check booth on the way into arrivals. I'm visiting ancient archaeological sites, I told her. How long will you be in Israel for? For 9 days, I'm going home December 24th. And so it went on again, the whole kit and kaboodle. I was handed back my passport and ticket, and I walked around the corner towards a gap in the cordoning fence, where a policewoman stood blocking my path. I handed her my passport and she paused with it briefly, but she didn't say "yer under arrest sugar!" She just passed it onto another military state lackey who asked me to step to one side and wait. They're very polite, these spooks. *He* walked over to somebody else who was dressed in a full suit and the two of them, plus a third party, went into a kind of a huddle.

Eventually the first fellow came back, then he ran through the gamut of identical questions all over again. Sometimes they came in different

forms, skirting around the back of one another in an attempt to trip me up, but I remained steadfast and smiling. He asked to see the accommodation booking reference a third time, and then he took it away to show to the man in the suit. They perused it together for five or ten minutes, whilst intermittently hassling a couple of Japanese tourists and a man in a Crocodile Dundee hat, who were being treated in a very similar manner: I wouldn't want you to think that I was alone in all of this. I think that they might well just hate everybody.
My government stalker came back over, still holding my accommodation booking reference. He didn't appear to have done anything with it.

"What else do you have in your bag, please sir?"
"Just some travel books on Israel, churches, something on local archaeology..." I explained, beginning to pull them out for him to see.
"OK, sir. It's OK" he reassured me. "Is this your only bag?"
"No, there's a bigger one over there on the carousel" I said, pointing over his shoulder at the now-distant baggage belt.
"OK sir. Wait here one moment please."

After I had been kept waiting for a while longer, I was informed that I would need to have my bag X-rayed again. I hung around for a further fifteen minutes before attempting to take the matter into my own hands. I walked over to where they were standing idly, in between harassing myself and Crocodile Dundee.

"Hello," I said. He turned around. "You wanted to X-ray my bag again?"
"Yes, your bag. Please bring it."

I walked over to where I had left the bag, next to the Japanese tourists. I was a little surprised that he hadn't even bothered to look through it, but he was now going to go to the trouble of sending it off somewhere to be X-rayed; but I didn't say anything. I guessed that it was all part of the game that I was reluctantly playing along with, out of sheer necessity. I walked over to hand it to him, but we had somehow crossed paths and he was now intimidating the two Japanese. I waited patiently for another five minutes, finally taking the initiative, and I touched him lightly on one elbow; he turned around.

"Excuse me. My bag. You wanted to X-ray it again?" I proffered him the day pack.
"You have only one bag?" he asked, seeming for just one moment to be genuinely confused.
"Oh, you want the other bag!" I suddenly exclaimed, finally catching on. "Right. OK. I'm just going over there now, OK, I'll be two minutes, alright, just two minutes!" I told him, holding two fingers up together in the air and trying my very best for them not to resemble an Intifada victory salute.

When I had at last come back with the damned thing, I was turned straight back around again with both bags and marched over to the X-ray machine, which turned out to be right next to the luggage carousel would you believe it. My twin items of battered old belongings were placed in what looked like a big red plastic bread tray, and then I was abandoned by his nibs and placed in the care of a third man, who looked like a tall gangly version of Brains from Thunderbirds. The bags must have come through cleanly enough because he handed me back the tray containing them without any questions. He asked me again for my passport and landing card, which acts as a discretionary visa application - usually allowing you either 1 month of 3 months stay - and then told me to follow him. I was close on his heels and before I knew it he was unlocking the door to an unmarked and deserted room. We walked into it and he bade me place the tray on the solitary table in the centre of the room. Then he asked to step straight into a barren, white and doorless cubicle. Right I thought, this is it, it's up-the–bum time. But it wasn't to be. He didn't follow me in there, and as soon as I was in he called me straight back out again. I think that there may have been a flashing LED set into one of the prefabricated walls, but I really can't be sure now. I suspected that I was perhaps being surreptitiously photographed, but it all happened so quickly that there was just no way to tell. When I emerged he was busy typing my name, date of birth, passport number and return flight details into a computer database that was set into one of the walls. Then he told me that I could go, I mean *really* go, and he handed me back my passport as I had just finished shouldering my bags.

"Do you know where it is?" he asked me.
"Follow the green arrow?" I suggested, pointing at a large green arrow mounted on the wall.
"Yes. That's right."
And that was it. As I was walking through the corridor, I flicked through my passport and noticed that it had already been stamped with an entrance visa for a period of 3 months. I have absolutely no idea when this happened.

I emerged through the gate to a concourse that was a lot smaller than I had expected. Not much at all was going on. Slowly it dawned on me that it was a Saturday, the Jewish *Shabbat*, and I was at last in the very heart of the promised land. Nervously, and expecting now to be followed or at least filmed again, I was almost tip-toeing around the edge of yet another perimeter fence before I could see anybody whom I recognised. What if they had all left me behind? Or what if none of the others had managed to get through, and they were all now languishing in a high-security lounge, surrounded by Mossad and IDF[xii] gunmen, and waiting to be sent home on the next available flight? I had seen one of our party who had been present at the planning meeting in Stamford Hill, a young female journalist, making her way through with apparent ease as I had been recovering one of my bags from the carousel to be X-rayed. But I thought I recalled that she had had a German-sounding name, and I surmised that maybe she had relatives who lived in Israel as well. Concentrating on making my way through the small concourse at a very measured pace, I kept looking around myself for a place to get a coffee, but there was nowhere open other than the money-changers. I was desperate for some attention-diverting activity, desperate to appear normal, and my paranoia was in the ascendant. I jangled the metal Shekels in my pocket that my mother had given to me two years before, when I had first decided that I wanted to come to this awful place. She had been here with a Holy Land tour in 1983, when there had still been around 100 Israeli Shekels to the British pound. Finally, as if in a dream, I noticed some familiar faces standing in a tight group around their bags just a short distance away. I strode towards them, beginning to feel a bit relieved, but now concerned that we were even more noticeable as conspiratorial state-wreckers, people who had claimed not have known each other from Adam, Eve, Rachel or Isaac barely an hour before.

"What's happening, then?" I asked Liz, hoping that she would by now have shed her ignorance of me.
"Hello Ted." I felt my relief immediately grow and prosper. "Well..." My heart sank. I sensed that bad news was coming. I raised my eyebrows and leant in towards her. She was whispering. This was all, indeed, very conspiratorial behaviour.
"Yes?"
"The transport hasn't arrived yet and I think that we're a few people short" she whispered to me. "What about you? Did you get through OK?"
I looked at my watch and I noticed that we should have been picked up about forty-five minutes previously. That's just as well for me then, I thought rather selfishly. But according to our directives from the PCR[xiii], somebody was supposed to have been waiting for us at this point, or even as we emerged from our parallel grillings. There should have been someone clutching a card reading 'ATG (ISM).' The Alternative Tourism Group, based in the West Bank.
"Well, they kept me in for about half an hour in total. They just kept asking the same questions over and over, who was paying for my flight, where was I staying, all that business. You know," I told her, shrugging my shoulders.
"Did they strip-search you?"

"Nah."

I was still very conscious of what was, to my mind, our overt conspicuousness. There just didn't seem to be anybody else about. Suddenly a memory of my beginners' Spanish teacher, Fabiola, flashed through my mind. She was brandishing a flashlight. 'Como te llamas?' she yelled at me, grinning. 'De donde vives?'; possibly recalling her childhood in Peru. I noticed what I thought was a coffee machine over on the far side of the hall, and I pulled some of the 20-year old change out of my by-now clammy pocket.
"Is this stuff still legal tender?" I asked, turning to Angie Zelter, an anti-occupation activist who is usually described in the press as a 'veteran peace campaigner'. She fingered a couple of the metal bits that I proffered to her in my right palm, moving them around in the grimy sweat.

"Yes, I think they're OK Ted" she told me. I was glad that these people had remembered me. My heart rate slowed down a little; Angie sounded human and confident.
"Now that's a five…" she said slowly, pushing a five-Shekel piece with '5' written on it through the grease, "…and these are ones. Yes, they look alright!"

I wasn't quite sure whether she thought I was some kind of an idiot or not, and at that point I really didn't care. I just wanted some coffee. There are worse things in the world, I'm sure. I thanked her and strode off towards what I took to be a coin-operated drinks dispensing machine.

Angie Zelter is an extraordinary woman. She was one of the 'Trident Three', who helped to temporarily disable the radar guidance equipment for the Trident nuclear weapons system, stationed on an MOD barge on Loch Goil at the Faslane base in Scotland in 1999. At her trial she represented herself, while the other two women opted for professional barristers. They were all acquitted, based on their defence that they were not so much committing a crime as acting to prevent a far greater one. The New Labour Mafiosi were terrified of the example that this might set for people's disarmament but, as they couldn't be tried again because of 'Double Jeopardy', it was forced to invoke a Lord Advocate's Reference. This is an extremely rare legal procedure that only served to highlight both the establishment's desperation, and the sham that the Scottish legal system or Assembly are in any way independent of Westminster, for anybody who was in any doubt about this. Angie's Affinity Group also helped to trash a Hawk fighter jet destined for imminent sale to the US-sponsored Indonesian government in 1996, for use in its genocidal campaign against the civilian population of East Timor. On this charge, which amounted to 'criminal damage' to the jet to the tune of about £1.5 million, there was an acquittal on similar grounds after 6 months spent in prison on remand. But you might not think this if you met her. There's no fanfare, and it's never mentioned or even alluded to. I only found out all of this by reading her book, 'TRIDENT ON TRIAL', months after having met her, and I only found out about that by sheer accident. Unassuming is not the word. She is fiercely opposed to the superficial cult of personality that pervades everything in our sick, six-second society but this is something that many people pay lip service to and are subsequently seduced by, without even noticing it. She is a woman in black who regularly travels all over the world to protest against war in all its forms and give educational talks.

Well, either the coffee machine didn't work, or else I simply couldn't understand it: naturally enough, all the prices and instructions were displayed in Hebrew script only. Eventually our driver arrived with his list. If your name's not down you ain't getting in, he implied. But we weren't all there, as they say. A couple of us elected to wait outside with him, while the three or four others remaining stayed inside the arrivals hall, to act as a beacon and look out for any stragglers or latecomers.

Then my German-sounding journalist, Alex, turned up, all beams and smiles. She had neither been detained by the authorities, nor had she disappeared off to some far-flung settlement in the Negev to see her Uncle Leviticus; she'd just been over to the other side of the airport, attempting to hire a mobile phone for the fortnight. This, apparently, can be quite a lengthy and arduous process. During the flight over, she had said hello to me, waved, and generally attempted to attract my attention and I had more or less ignored her, out of my unflinching pragmatism. Now I just felt silly. But it's a hard revolution, and you have to be tough.

She was accompanied by Saleyha Ahsan, another journalist who was making a documentary on the Women In Black for BBC radio 5, and her sound man. The sun was getting low in the sky by now, burning the top off the horizon. I looked around at the expected mix of big American pickup trucks and palm trees, appreciating the last of the dying Mediterranean December warmth. Our driver began checking names off his list, and was left with only one missing person, who was due in on a later flight from the United States. We stood around smoking cigarettes and chewing gum for a while longer, and every so often the airport police would come and speak to the driver and he would have to drive around the block a couple of times. Then, before too much longer, Jordan - our missing link - emerged from the lounge, and Angie and Liz too. There were more smiles. Everything seemed to be coming together at last.

"Alright there?" somebody asked Jordan. "Safe journey?"
"Yeah…" he began, rubbing at the corners of his eyes. "Well, I actually left my apartment almost 24 hours ago…"
"Where are you from?"
"New York City."

There was a bit of a silence at that point, punctuated by the odd unspoken 'wow', a hangover from the still-recent events of September 11th of that year. This, of course, was when the World Trade Centre in lower Manhattan had been completely destroyed by anonymous terrorists, killing upwards of 3,000 people. This had prompted the US administration to all but declare total war on the independent Arab world, in a cynical pursuit of the domination of future oilfields, and in the form of unending revenge attacks for the obliteration of its symbol of the subjugation of the third world. By which I mean the rest of us. My attitude may shock many people, and my feelings and my sympathies are constantly with the relatives of so many fire service workers, restaurant staff, cleaners and other perennially underpaid service sector employees who perished in that abhorrent catastrophe. But this was surely a building out of which much of the causes of suffering and inequality in the world emanated. Jordan's e-mail address, by the way, is 'anticapitalist' and he's a young trade union organiser. I never did get around to asking him specifically how he felt about it all, or whether or not he'd lost any friends or colleagues in there.

But now we were completo. It was almost dark as we set out on our way to Beit Sahour.

Unlike most Palestinian 'Servis'[xiv] journeys around Gaza and the West Bank, our initial one was very straightforward. Being an international tourist agency, the ATG have a pristine van with yellow (i.e. Israeli) license plates. This means that they are allowed to travel with relative ease along the main roads and national highways that criss-cross Israel and the West Bank, and which even serve to bisect the Gaza strip. Most Palestinians, on the other hand, have only either white or green plates: and so they must find other, much more roundabout routes, which can turn a potential 45-minute road journey into one of three or more hours. Some Gazans have even been known, during the long closures of the strip, to travel to work in Israel via Egypt and then Jordan and the Allenby Bridge, where the likelihood of being refused passage is considerably lower.

Saleyha began recording her radio programme, beginning a series of short interviews with Liz. Liz talked about the high-speed route that we were taking across the breadth of Israel at what is almost its widest point, a short distance of some 40 or so miles along a modern highway that had been paid for in American tax dollars and expropriated Palestinian farmland. As we drove over the hills and down through the valleys of the centre of Palestine at a very convenient speed, a luxury that is denied to almost all native Palestinians, we were able to see the lights of the nearby settlements and other Israeli towns. I chatted away rather forcedly to Angie on this first evening, questioning her half-heartedly on her religious views and her previous experience of this poor beleaguered country, as I felt the demands of the day began to catch up with me and we approached the relative sanctuary of Beit Sahour.

Less than three-quarters of an hour later we had skirted the edge of Jerusalem and were gingerly approaching the Bethlehem checkpoint, which was staffed by a lone IDF conscript. Much to my surprise, and contrary to so many of those ubiquitous tales of terror from the occupation, we barely had to stop on our way through. A few words were exchanged between the soldier and our driver and then we were on our way. No identification had been requested from us, and the pair of them were quite probably known to one another. But such situations can become reversed in the twinkling of an eye, and nothing out here should be taken for granted. For example, there is the well-known (amongst ISM regulars) case of the IDF soldier who works at the military checkpoint that's on the northern side of Jerusalem on the main road heading up-country towards the West Bank city of Ramallah. He could regularly be observed sporting a CND symbol, along with the word 'PEACE', etched in biro onto the fabric band of his army helmet. Most of the time he would appear very friendly, indeed almost gregarious, toward the peace activists and even to some Palestinians as well, whilst in their presence. But at other times he was to be seen threatening civilians quite openly and very violently. On the one occasion that I was able to personally observe him, he had tucked a card into the band of his helmet to obscure the offending graffito, doubtless under specific instructions from his commanding officer.

The first thing that you notice when you leave the Jewish section of east Jerusalem, and hence 'Israel proper', is the instant deterioration of the quality of the roads and the street lighting. In fact, all manner of infrastructure all over both the West Bank and the Gaza strip are chronically both under-developed and maintained. I was to discover this later, when I attempted to use an internet connection at the Ararat hotel, close to where we would be staying for our first couple of nights. As we hastened away from Bethlehem checkpoint it immediately became very much darker, and yet at the same time miniature dust storms were clearly visible, billowing rapidly in and out of view. I had also thought that the London Borough of Hackney must surely have held the world record for its number of atrocious potholes. Yet here was a tiny part of the reality of the occupation: at any moment I felt that we might go careening off the road and into the side of a house, bringing our speedy progress into one of the centres of world peace activism to an abrupt halt.

There was at least a cursory welcoming committee to greet us when we alighted from our servis at the Three Kings hotel. Georgina Reeves is a young middle-class woman from London, who was previously employed in the city, in the business sector there. Now she works mainly for the Palestine Centre for Rapprochement and lives in Beit Sahour, as she had done for the past year. She told me that she had come to Palestine because she felt that her life and her job at home had no real meaning; and that she now rarely goes into Israel, because of the ignorance and the terrible anti-Arab bigotry that she finds there.

Our baggage was carried inside for us and we made our way up the first flight of stairs into the dining area, where tea and coffee were waiting for us on tap. Perfecto. The hotel was new and had been near to completion when the second Intifada erupted, putting the dampers on the final touches of the construction work. As a consequence the elevators weren't functioning; but this was no real inconvenience. We were the first booking that the hotel had had for over a year. The rooms were immaculate and from my balcony I could clearly see the empty settlement perched on a nearby hill, with the putrescent yellow light of the IDF protection outpost close by it. There are some 35,000 brand-new apartments standing idle at Har Homa, but because of its extremely vulnerable position no settlers have been found to inhabit them as yet; so the army merely uses its position to shell the community of Beit Sahour during what are no doubt seen as opportune moments in the uprising.

My room-mate for the next couple of nights was to be Chris Dunham, another of those who had been present at our planning meeting. "Tee-ed!" he hailed me, as I was just getting settled in for the night and beginning to worry about my dinner. "How's it go-ing?"

We exchanged further pleasantries and I ascertained that he had already been in the area for a couple of days, had spent the afternoon and evening hanging out in the Old City of Jerusalem, and was consequently already well-fed and watered. I outlined for him my slight difficulties with the immigration people at Ben Gurion, and I remarked that I wouldn't have dared attempting to get through carrying the book that he was reading, Noam Chomsky's '*World Orders, old and new.*' After I had completely unpacked my meagre resources I made my way back down to the hotel lobby to snatch a much-needed cigarette. From there I quickly managed to attach myself to an ad-hoc grouping of other newcomers, who had managed to solicit a ride down the hill from the ATG transport to a nearby eaterie.

The restaurant turned out to be a large Bedouin tent, constructed from large sheathes of sacking material and with gas heaters burning all around. The evening cold was now rapidly drawing in around us: December is the rainy season in the West Bank, and although it wasn't raining at that moment I had come ill prepared for it. It had been pleasantly warm in Tel Aviv and I was expecting more of the same, but this was not to be. The waiters dressed as waiters do throughout most of the world, the only real difference being that, due to the occupation and the closures, most of the main courses on the menu were unavailable. Not to worry, I thought. You will often find this in Wood Green also, and we instead contented ourselves with a sumptuous array of vegetarian mezze.

There was almost nobody else in there, and half of our group either appeared to be, or had been in the past, schoolteachers. Personally I had a terrible time in school, where it seemed to me that the teachers were enthusiastically colluding with the school bullies to humiliate and degrade my every waking moment. At times it seemed as though they were working a double-shift system side by side. Now my comrades-to-be were endlessly talking shop, with one of them in particular taking me back to those dark places that we all have inside us somewhere, some large and some small, like a little septic tank at the back of the brain that we dare not empty because the smell is so bad. The kids that I have to teach, she said, oh my god it's such a trial, I should never have to go through it. I really know about suffering, I do. They don't even want to learn anything, and they're so thick anyway, because they've never even heard of the classics. Of course what they really need is a good kicking, she implied. But they're so damn dumb that they probably wouldn't feel anything anyway. I kept on sucking down my hummus and Russian salad with rubber peas, grinding my teeth and mentally reminding myself that it takes all sorts of people to make a real and lasting change. Particularly as this same person is now working tirelessly in the London Jewish community to foment debate over Palestinian human rights and the future, if there can be one, of political Zionism. But my abiding memory of her for quite a while was of when we had kindly been put up in a house in the Bir Zeit vicinity, saying that she had paid her $3 for breakfast and she was expecting more than a couple of pieces of fruit. All sorts of people. Together.

Another of the teachers was Rod Quinn, a middle-aged writer and a PSC member who's originally from rural western Australia. He's a lifelong socialist who is currently working on biographies of Thomas Mann and one of the Pankhurst sisters, and the original Australian 1960s man. In fact, he had lived in Palestine for a couple of years all that time ago, from 1962 until 1964. He seemed a little perturbed that he couldn't get his barbecued meat on this occasion, but he cheerfully put it all down to the closures and chomped down the veg, chips pitta bread and sauces with the rest of us. Later he would elaborate on the more pressing implications of Israel's economic blockade of Gaza and the West Bank in PSC's monthly magazine '*Palestine News*':

"The closure bears heavily on the rural communities. Many villages are under virtual siege with all entry roads sealed by roadblocks. Yasuf, one such village, supported our decision to clear the barriers from their main road-link to the outside world. From the outset it was clear, because of the many large concrete blocks forming the barrier, that our action would be limited. We were able, however, to exploit a large enough gap between the blocks and were jubilant after watching a token crossing by a village vehicle. The army arrived as our work was almost completed and we involved them in discussions while we linked up in some sort of human chain. We were told that we would be unable to return to our accommodation because Marda, our host village, was now declared a closed military zone – despite 2,000 Palestinian men, women and children still 'living' inside it. We did later make our way back there, however, to our welcoming hosts. A particularly malicious tactic used by the occupation forces is to erect two roadblocks separated by 50 yards or so, as in Yasuf. This means that supplies coming into the village must be carried between the barriers. When there is only one barrier as in Deir Istya where we were able to form a chain and help, the supplies can be transferred directly from the delivery truck to one inside the roadblock.'

But more of that later. For the time being we were all but exhausted, particularly Jordan after his 18-hour flight from New York, who said little during our first limited experience of typical Palestinian cuisine. We were, however, able to converse a little during our walk back up Arafat Street to the hotel. In the main, we were just a little amazed to be here at last; to be finally in a position to do something other than simply gawp in unbelieving horror at the daily scenes of ethnic cleansing and human misery unfolding on our TV screens back at home.

Settle Down...

The failure of the so-called 'peace process', even if you discount completely its complete abandonment of the 1948 refugees, lies in its inability to address the issue of the illegal settlements: if you want to know the reasons behind the second Intifada then look no further than the fact that these they have doubled in population since 1993. Israel builds them on hilltops overlooking centuries-old Palestinian villages and towns. Their occupants receive grants, homes, vehicles, gun licenses and possibly even immigration expenses as well. There is always an IDF post or base close by 'to protect them', and before you know it the army have sealed off most of the indigenous centres of population nearby for 'security purposes'. This means that the villagers can't get food and other essential supplies in and out, not to mention ambulances or other emergency vehicles. Sometimes you'll see a supply truck backed up to a roadblock, with another brought up from inside the beleaguered village to the opposite side of the roadblock, and its contents transferred by hand. Then the army come in at night with their Caterpillar bulldozers, doubling or trebling-up the roadblock and making this impossible. Meanwhile the government will have built a modern highway to the settlement, which Palestinians aren't allowed to drive on. The settlers sporadically vandalise the farmland the Palestinians can no longer get to, and attack them if they try. Here again, they are protected by the IDF. After six months or a year the army applies to the courts to confiscate the land for 'military purposes', arguing that it is 'uncultivated': such a request will be invariably granted by an Israeli judge, and in time it'll be handed over to the settlement.

'..during the seven years of the Oslo process, Israel doubled its Jewish settlement population in the West Bank and Gaza to almost 200,000. In East Jerusalem it grew to 170,000. More than 18,330 new housing units were constructed, according to the Israeli Bureau of Statistics, and thousands of dunams of Palestinian land were confiscated to expand the settlements'[xv], explains the Israeli human rights lawyer Allegra Pachecho in a recent article.

But these settlements have to begin somewhere, and this generally takes the form of a small number of mobile homes, lean-tos, and tents positioned on a hillside overlooking viable Palestinian land and resources. In June 2001, Neta Golan, a committed Israeli peace activist who is married to a Palestinian, and is occasionally quoted as being the 'founder of the ISM', had her arm broken by Israeli police at the village of El-Khader. New settlement caravans had been set up on a hillside overlooking the village, and to oppose them a protest tent was maintained for fifteen days and nights. On June 14th the tent was confiscated by the military (despite it being on the villagers' land), and the following morning a temporary shelter replaced it. At 2pm negotiations began and the activists were given ten minutes in which to make their speeches. Once again, the area had become a 'closed military zone'. Arik Ascherman, the director of Rabbis for Human Rights, called upon both the soldiers and the police to recognise that they had come in peace, Israelis and Palestinians alike[xvi]. The military said that they didn't want any trouble either, armed as they were with their M16 assault rifles and all wearing bullet-proof vests.

After 25 minutes some people had already started to move away. Suddenly the police rushed down the hill at the demonstrators, seizing many of them and placing them under arrest after beating them with their batons. Neta had already been hit several times when she had her arm pulled up behind her back. Another policeman then grabbed the arm and twisted it up to the level of her neck; Neta says that at this point, she heard 'popping noises' and she knew that something had snapped. She quietly requested medical attention for some two hours, during which time she was told by the police "You fell down, that is why you are hurt." They then threw her out of the police station, but she refused to leave until the other detainees were released as well, which they then were. Five hours on from the time that she was injured, fellow activists got Neta to a hospital where she was told that her arm had indeed been broken at the elbow. Meanwhile, however, 24 soldiers continued chasing and shooting the villagers all of the way into the town. An hour after the initial police charge, five Palestinians had been shot and injured with rubber bullets and their temporary shelter was torn down, whilst "armed settlers roamed free and content" on the hillside.

While I was helping to dismantle a roadblock barring passage into the village of Yasuf in the Salfit area, a parallel crew were doing likewise at the nearby Kefl Hares. However, unfortunately for both themselves and the villagers, their obstruction was a lot larger and taller than ours was and they had only managed to dismantle about half of it when settler police turned up and began to make life difficult for them. Several settlers had halted their cars to yell abuse, but work was still going on when suddenly two enormous settlers came running around the corner, yelling abuse and kicking, punching and lashing out in all directions. They assaulted two activists, but fortunately the police intervened very quickly. It took several police and soldiers to restrain and handcuff them and they were dragged off, still protesting that they were innocent, that God had given them the land, and that it was the peace activists that the police ought to have been arresting. It should be noted that these are settler police who ought to have no jurisdiction whatsoever in a Palestinian village. If the arrested men ever have to stand up in court then that court will be within the settlement, where the judge will be a settler just like them, and probably known to them personally.

The next day, the army sent a bulldozer to restore the roadblock. A young Palestinian-American woman, Sofia Ahmad from Bir Zeit University, threw herself in front of it running and screaming, and covered head to toe in red Palestinian mud. She was arrested for a few hours and taken to a police station within the settlement [Ariel], but later released.

Can there be any hope of peace between Israeli settlers and Palestinian villagers, or is this just naïve? The image that the settlers have in both the popular and the radical press internationally, whilst it might be slightly more deserved, is at least half as bad as that of Palestinian militants and suicide bombers. In the interests of balance and just finding things out for themselves, Women In Black stalwarts Liz Khan and Hanna Braun[xvii] – accompanied by the BBC radio 5 reporter Saleyha Ahsan – ventured into Gush Etzion settlement, near Hebron, to talk to some of its residents and to try to get their heads around why anybody would actually *want* to live in what is also for them, effectively, a state of siege. Why would anyone choose to live in a war zone?

Sheryl is a resident of Gush Etzion, a transplanted Jewish Canadian. 'The feeling in my community is that we're not getting equal time,' she told Saleyha. 'Come and see what it's like. We're not like these gun-toting, aggressive, hateful settlers. What we are is we're regular people. We can probably have the same taste in music. Am I your image of a settler? Why not? Why am I not your image of a settler?' she asks Liz.

'You haven't fitted that image, but I have to say that I have met people who have fitted that image. I have been spat at by Israelis,' Liz replies in a patient and very conciliatory tone.
'But why? What were you doing? What were you doing?' Sheryl comes back straight away, very defensively. The implication is that if you were around here, and we don't know you, and you aren't one of us, then you have to be a dangerous threat. Even though we've only been here for 34 years, and even though our internationally-illegal nationhood is wholly based on fear, terror and a dubious mythology.
'I was with a tour, walking through Hebron' Liz says, 'and I walked up to Abraham's tomb and I was spat at.'
'Were you carrying a sign?'
'No, we weren't doing anything.'

'I suspect that if you sat down with those ladies who spat at you – because I know them – that you would find them as intelligent and as reasonable as you find me' Sheryl replies, without so much as a hint of irony.

Ariel is a luxurious hilltop settlement of over 16,000 Zionist Jews. When its namesake, Israeli Prime Minister Ariel Sharon visited it, he announced that it was the Biblical Samaria. The area is of course confiscated land that was previously used by Palestinian farmers for growing olives, wheat and barley. The water for the settlement, including that for Jewish swimming pools, is taken from the nearby Palestinian villages where the population now suffers from a dire shortage of water.[xviii] Wadi Kanaa, for example, is a scenic area of freshwater springs and a major water source. It is now seriously polluted by sewage and industrial effluent from the settlement. We stopped our coach by the roadside to climb down a muddy bank, to investigate what ostensibly appeared to be a sewage-treatment facility for the religious settlement that towered above us. But it was no such thing. All that we found there was a tatty fence surrounding a waste pipe that constantly spilled every conceivable variety of effluent and junk into the Palestinian's water supply, effectively murdering it. The terrain underfoot was now a stinking black gunge, and everywhere there was the general stench of overwhelming decay. After the initial wave of amazement at the sheer stupidity of it all had subsided a little, we couldn't wait to clean off our boots and get back onto the bus.

Because of this, many Palestinians have lost their land and their livelihood and now instead provide cheap labour for the settlers. Settlements in the West Bank are all connected to one another by the well-maintained settler-only roads, of course. Israel's initial excuse for them is that, under Oslo and the concomitant Declaration of Principles, they are necessary in order to facilitate the speedy evacuation of its army from the occupied territories.[xix] This is called 'redeployment'; but the IDF doesn't appear to be going anywhere. And until it does, until Israel finally withdraws its monumental US-funded war machine to behind the green line, then the Intifada will resurface again and again. And again. Until there is finally justice for the Palestinian people, and with it the peace that everybody says that they want.

Training day

The next morning we were up bright and early at 8am for a lukewarm shower, and lots of instant coffee for breakfast. There was plenty more food as well, but I can never eat breakfast, a lingering reminder of my drinking days. When I got downstairs I found a sea of faces, both familiar and otherwise. I sat down with Chris, and Rachel Boyd and Joe Button who are fellow Hackney compadres, and my last two links from the Stamford Hill meeting. They share a houseboat on Hackney's urban river, the Lee, and they cook a mean risotto. Rachel's grandmother was a German Jew who fled the nazis in the 1930s to come to Britain, but her parents are both Quakers, as is she. She's a signatory to the Trident Ploughshares pledge, which confers on her a certain responsibility to resist and act against the international war machine wherever possible, and she has been attending political demonstrations for as long as she can remember, ever since her childhood. Despite - or perhaps even because of - all of this she spent a large portion of her time in Palestine in West Jerusalem and other Jewish enclaves, travelling around with the affinity group 'Junity' and getting back in touch with her history. Junity are in fact a very active wider organisation, essentially of Jewish-Americans, who seek to explore ways of co-ordinating the efforts of the many Jewish organisations working for a just and lasting peace between Israelis and Palestinians.

It only seemed as though only ten minutes or so had passed, and I was still wiping the sleep from around my eyes, when well-organised phalanxes of spry activists began noisily scraping chairs back and forth, creating three concentric semicircles of seating that faced a television, video recorder and a basic sound system. To the best of my knowledge, none of these were ever used for group purposes. But the arrangement did provide a handy focus for the speakers who were to address us with their informative, inspiring, and occasionally disconcerting wit over the next couple of days.

The first up was Huwaida Arraf, a Palestinian-American who lives in Ramallah with her fiancé Adam Shapiro, also an American citizen. Along with others, they had organised the fortnight of actions that we were now about to participate in. Huwaida outlined the programme of events over the coming days, emphasising that everything was subject to change at short notice, all of this according to the constantly-changing local situation. For example, we were supposed to have been tree-planting for two days, but this had to be cancelled because of poor weather conditions.

This activity is not so innocuous and earth-motherly as it at first sounds. As a result of the closures of almost all Palestinian villages in the current situation, the villagers are unable to get to and therefore cultivate their farmland. There is generally an illegal Zionist settlement close by on the nearest hill as I have mentioned, and there will be forays by the Jewish settlers to uproot and vandalise the crops (most usually Olive trees) at night and at other times. IDF bulldozers and jeeps will, more often than not, also be involved in this wanton destruction. After this has been going on for some time, say for example for a year, the IDF apply to the Israeli courts to confiscate the land for what they term 'military uses'. This will sound like quite reasonable grounds for sequestration of property to an Israeli judge. After a little more time has elapsed, the land will be given over into the hands of the settlement when the army say that they've finished with it, and the settlers will then farm it as their own. So then, the replanting of trees by the agricultural land's rightful owners, which is essentially the reclaiming of stolen land, becomes a very dangerous activity as the land tends to be quite a way from any easily-navigable roads for the army, police and emergency services. Whilst you might not normally wish to be left to the mercy of the Israeli police or the IDF, they at least have an official code of conduct to which they ought to adhere: there is of course no such set of guidelines for illegal settlers. Thus, in helping the Palestinians in this way, you are essentially at the mercy of armed and quite often fanatically-religious Zionists who are a law unto themselves. They will attack you, threaten to kill your Palestinian friends in front of you, and spit at you. They will fire live ammunition into the air and at the ground very close to your feet, tell you that you're a nazi, that the Christians killed the Jews, and that this land was given to them by God in the Bible. There is, of course, very little reasoning with such arguments – particularly when they're being screamed at you in Hebrew in a non-stop ten-minute tirade and a flurry of spittle – but your silence might well indicate your guilt, and therefore your complicity in the nazi holocaust, to such an irate believer. It ought still to be mentioned that even such devout bigots will be mindful of the consequences of shooting an international peace activist, and that this was extremely unlikely to happen to any of us, even non-fatally. But I imagine that it would still be very scary.

The non-violent guidelines were then presented to us, and we were asked to adhere to them at all times. These included an undertaking not to be drunk or under the influence of drugs, other than for medical purposes, at all times. There was also the promise never to use violence, or even any threatening or abusive language, to anybody at all. Although we might find certain aspects of the local culture to be anomalous with our presumably egalitarian beliefs, we were not here to foist cultural imperialism or even political enlightenment upon anybody, and we should behave with the utmost respect towards everyone with whom we made contact, even the soldiers. At this stage Neta Golan, another of the principal organisers, stood up to explain that although we would all have our own reasons for being present for the fortnight's activities, and some of us even our own agendas, these should all be left at home. We were here to help the Palestinian people in their plight, and to assist in bringing this plight to the attention of the wider world. Particularly it was stressed that, as few of us had to live in Palestine, we had no right whatsoever – even as peace activists - to criticise the Palestinian people if they chose to fight the occupation 'with weapons'; and that as none of us had had to grow up through it all our lives, nor had we probably lost our homes and our entire families because of it, it wasn't really possible for us to empathise to such an extent as to enable us to judge. There were no dissenting voices at all to this, and a general feeling of agreement toward the sentiments expressed.

Following the programme details, registration was explained. We all had to pay around $350 for our accommodation, for food and for transport costs. This seemed to me to be a very reasonable amount for the time that we would be spending there and the distances that we would have to cover in that time. Then we were asked to organise, those of us that had not done so previous to coming out, into Affinity Groups.

The Affinity Group was something that had been nominally explained to me at Stamford Hill. So far as I was aware, it began with the American 'Plowshares' movement, and involved small autonomous groupings within the whole, usually with between six and ten people in each one. The purpose of the affinity groups is to get to know each other more intimately in a short space of time, and thus to better facilitate our looking out for one another at foreseeable crisis points during actions. For example, if during a march we were attacked by the IDF with disorientating sound grenades and tear gas, and then baton rounds[xx] or even live ammunition were discharged and there were some arrests in the confusion, it would be much easier to account for any missing persons within these smaller groups and then to report back to the whole, in a calm and rational manner. Each affinity group would have its own press contact, first aid officer, a jail solidarity contact and so forth. For practical reasons, these people would generally be designated as 'non-arrestable', although of course this is not often a matter of choice. At the end of each day, one representative from each affinity group would attend a meeting of what was called the 'spokes-council', which also comprised two delegates from the organisers, who had decided to call themselves the 'leadership group'. This raised a few sniggers from some of us of a certain political persuasion but, at least in my own AG, it was decided that we didn't really care what they wanted to call themselves, at least until a specific problem arose from their handling of the daily affairs. Each group was also to give itself a name, silly or otherwise. We were to be called the 'tapdancers', a peculiar acronym the roots of which I don't care to remember. At any spare moment it was considered prudent that we get into our individual AG's and talk through whatever was going on at the time.

There was some more coffee, and next up to speak was Val Phillips, a very knowledgeable and pragmatic medical officer who told us all about how to avoid and minimise the harmful effects of the tear gas, sound grenades, and bullets that we should all at least expect to encounter at some point during our stay. Val had come as part of a delegation from Colorado in the United States, all of whom worked tirelessly, day and night, on their media work and put the rest of us to shame. For those who are interested, they have an extensive web site diary of the ISM's activities in Palestine during December-January 2001/2002, which is available at www.ccmep.org/palestine, and is surely the definitive article on that fortnight. Val and Mark Schneider, also from Colorado, had also managed to raise the whole of the funds for their group's excursion half way across the world virtually single-handedly.

A sound – or "percussion" – grenade is another thing that is not nearly so innocuous as it might at first seem. Its primary purpose is to disorientate and disperse any gathering, and according to IDF regulations it ought to be fired into the air, and above the heads of its intended victims. However, the IDF being the IDF, this is often not the practice. If it lands on the ground next to you, you ought to cover it with some item of heavy clothing if this is at all possible, and then strive to protect your ears. It is intended to induce panic; so it must be stressed that its effects are largely in your own hands. Having said this however, should you pick it up in an attempt to get rid of it and it goes off in your hand, you'll probably lose a couple of fingers. An instance was also related of a sound bomb exploding close to somebody's leg while they were on the ground, and that person then had bruises imprinted on their thigh in the shape of the change in his pocket for about a month.

Several spent sound bombs were passed around for the purposes of familiarisation, along with two different examples of empty tear gas canisters, the remains of one of which took the form of some shredded strips of black plastic, with traces of a noxious black powder still slightly in evidence. Hand washing was strongly recommended in this case. Also distributed for our perusal were two different types of baton rounds. My idea of a baton round ("It smashes heads!") was of a large, very hard plastic projectile that could quite easily kill you if aimed at your head from close range: but these things seemed to be even worse, if anything. Of two different sizes, both of which appeared to be very big to me, these were simply a solid steel slug encased in a thin sheet of rubber. At both ends the essential projectile was clearly visible, whether the thing had been previously fired or not. It wasn't difficult to see why the daily death tolls of Palestinian schoolchildren in Gaza and the West Bank were, and are, so abominably high.

This was getting interesting - if a little unnerving - very fast. Before I knew it, we were on to techniques for dealing with the tear gas. Val explained, with the help of several veterans of the Seattle street uprisings of November/December 1999, that the best way of keeping tear gas at bay is with a handkerchief, a rag, or a scarf that has been previously soaked in vinegar. There is something in the vinegar that counteracts the gas, she explained, although nobody seemed to know quite what that something was. Directly inhaling vinegar fumes is not something that I would recommend that you do for kicks, but it is infinitely preferable to the effects of toxic gas, which is what tear gas is. Contrary to conventional wisdom, the effects of these chemical weapons are not always confined to fifteen or so minutes of intense pain and incapacitation. Prolonged exposure can result in permanent liver or lung damage, organ failure, "or even death"[xxi]. In the short or immediate term, the effects of the nausea and the disorientation engendered by these obnoxious compounds can be absolutely terrifying.[xxii] And all this from a form of domestic crowd control that would be illegal in time of war.[xxiii]

It was also stipulated that the best defence against the effects of the gas would be to avoid it as much as possible. Whilst this might sound like a fanciful notion given the likelihood of its deployment, useful tactics could be staying close to the ground, working out the direction of the prevailing wind beforehand, and discarding any contaminated clothing where practicable. Closing one's eyes for the whole period of any assault was deemed to be essential, although the wearing of swimming goggles as a mode of protection was not recommended as gas may become trapped behind the lenses, possibly giving rise to permanent eye damage. A demonstration was also given of eye-flushing techniques for medical officers, at which point Tommy stood up and spoke of his experiences of the use of tear gas for crowd control in the North of Ireland in the 1980s. Tommy had had a wealth of experience in dealing with such circumstances. He told us that standard procedure there when people on a demonstration were marching in a line was that once a person becomes contaminated, then that person moves downwind to the end of the line so that nobody else is infected, and the whole march proceeds calmly as before.

It had been a very rewarding first morning, and we adjourned for lunch to a restaurant just around the corner. Once more, the fare for us vegetarians was a sumptuous mezze, and I sat down to dine with Brian, another US citizen and organiser, and Ghassan, a young Palestinian man who has lived in Beit Sahour all of his life. A great talker, Ghassan was a little confused by the concept of vegetarianism given all the things that he had seen in his short life. In a later e-mail to me, he remarked: "I remember you – you are the veg guy!" Then he went on to tell us something of his experiences.

"The circumstances that brought me into this campaign were that I wanted to have my freedom. I have watched as the occupation continues to destroy my country. It's the dream of every Palestinian to have freedom and to live in peace. The Israeli army killed my best friend and my cousin as they sat in his house watching TV, so I want this occupation and this war to end now. I choose non-violence because I want to live in peace, and I don't believe that killing people is the right way to achieve our aims. I don't like to see people killing each other, but I also cannot say that those who choose to fight the occupation with weapons are wrong; they just have their own way of fighting the occupation, one that differs from mine."

I told Ghassan that even in the progressive-liberal British mainstream press, I had read that 70% of the Palestinian people supported the suicide bombers. How true was this, I wanted to know. And what did he think about it?

"I say the Israelis brought this on themselves, because if you look at the lives of the suicide bombers you'll see that the Israelis have either taken his land, or they've killed his brother or his friend or his father. In Palestine the Israeli army kills people because they are Palestinians. I think that is the reason why 70% of Palestinians are supporting the suicide bombers."

I told him that I had been at first in two minds about coming out to Palestine to be with the ISM, given the historic role of Britain in facilitating the creation of the state of Israel.

"I think the British role in building Israel did have some effect on Palestinians in their fight against the occupation, but that's all in the past now and we now have to be conciliatory and peaceful. We have to have respect from others too, respect that we are a people who want to live a free life and not to die at the hands of Israel's army. We need this support from our friends in this war.

I have to say that we as Palestinians love peace, and we want to live in peace, but this peace has to give us our freedom and our state, as all people in the world enjoy. We are not terrorists, we just want freedom, justice and dignity in our country. Freedom in Palestine."

The sun was shining brightly, and although it seemed a shame to go back inside on such a beautiful day there were still a great many things to get through. The next people to address us were Leanne and Rick, two Americans who were currently resident and active in Hebron with the CPT[xxiv]. CPT have activists all over the world; it's an organisation committed to reducing violence by "Getting in the Way" – challenging systems of domination and exploitation, as Jesus Christ did in the first century. They offer an organised, non-violent alternative to war and other forms of lethal inter-group conflict. CPT provides organisational support to persons committed to faith-based non-violent alternatives, in situations where lethal conflict is an immediate reality or is supported by pubic policy. In Hebron their main objective seems to lie in attempting to engage to some degree with the Zionist settlers, and in protecting Palestinian civilians from their volatile wrath. The tension that seems to pervade this town - which even the Lonely Planet Guide describes as "wholly Arab"[xxv] - at all times, centres around the settlement of Kiryat Arba, situated right on the edge of town. The travel guide goes on to tell us that:
'Blatantly provocative, the 400 strong Hebron settler community has gone on record saying that it's their desire to see the Arabs driven out of Hebron. As protection from the overwhelming majority of Palestinians among whom they live, the settlers are guarded by some 2500 Israeli soldiers and police with numerous roadblocks, checkpoints and concrete barricades.' The Jewish claim to the town goes back to the Book of Genesis[xxvi].

Leanne told us about how the settlers see 'outsiders'. 'When they see you, first they'll go into a kind of a huddle. Then they'll start to kind of bounce,' she said, physically illustrating this to much amusement. 'You might laugh, but it's true! You wait. You'll see, if you go there!' She went on to describe how we would then likely be treated, and Neta walked up to take on the role of a settler. We would be spat upon, called nazis, informed that we had killed the Jews, and possibly many worse things besides. In other words, all of the usual stuff. This could lead us to feel disempowered, humiliated, undoubtedly speechless, and very possibly quite enraged. But it was always best to simply say nothing, and to let them vent their spleen for about ten minutes. Possible verbal defences, such as 'It wasn't me, I wasn't born until 1966!' were seen as being wholly counter-productive. When the settlers had run out of energy, they would go back into their huddle and quite possibly begin the process all over again. It seemed as if there was nothing we could do. I must admit that I felt a little confused at this point, wondering what – in that case – our point in being there was. But Hebron has become an awful place for racist anti-Palestinian violence and murder, and my feelings now are that we ought to be there, if only to show support and solidarity with the Palestinian people in their struggle against this gross and obvious injustice.

Next up was a role-play exercise, which meant getting into line. One line was made up of the more experienced activists, who faced a parallel line of the rest of us. The experienced people played the role of IDF soldiers who had just declared a Palestinian village to be a 'Closed Military Area', a frequent and arbitrary tactic requiring no real paperwork or authorisation. We were attempting to cross the army line and get to our Palestinian friends who were beyond them, and they were 'asking' us to leave. In such situations, the IDF have – in theory - no power of arrest over internationals, and must wait for the police to arrive. Our task was to stand our ground and remain calm, and I understood this to be a purely verbal exercise. However, my opposite number – Brian, whom I had met at lunchtime - had other ideas. He just screamed and screamed at me at first, whilst I explained that it was important that I reach my friends, pointing over his shoulder toward them. After a very short time he commenced pushing me violently in the chest, and before I knew it I was over on the other side of the room, far away from everybody else. Although I had clearly misread the situation, I felt that the exercise had been a success, as it had demonstrated to me what it might really be like on the ground in the days to follow, and had given me plenty to think about. There followed a similar exercise where I was interviewed by Brian, who in this case played a mainstream journalist. I had two minutes to explain to him what I thought I was doing in helping to dissemble an IDF roadblock blocking access into a local village, when the Israeli government had said that it was – as per usual – a nest of terrorists or some such tripe. In this instance I felt that I carried myself off a little better, I more or less made my point in the allotted time, and there was no shoving.

The last item on the day's agenda was a talk to be given by a local Catholic priest[xxvii], who was delayed in getting to us through a number of IDF checkpoints, for obvious reasons. The theme of the talk was the meaning of *Jihad* in Islam, and due to some language problems there were many further delays, and the talk went on for about 90 minutes. I'm afraid that many of us thought that the ground he covered was somewhat repetitive, not particularly instructive, and that the time could have been better spent in either other role-playing exercises or affinity group quality time.

The day was almost done, and I made my way across the road to the Ararat hotel, where they have a public restaurant and an internet café situated on the top floor. Following a cheese salad and chips and a brief conversation with members of the aptly–named 'Shoulder-to-Shoulder' Affinity group, I made my way into the café.

"OK, for you, as you eat here and it is your first time - it is free! Normally it's 3 Shekels for 30 minutes" the barman told me when I enquired as to whether I could use an internet connection. "Any machine!"

So far so good. I took my place among two or three other peace activists, and attempted to log on to the world wide web. Things were going a little slowly, but progressing OK: and the machine looked to be tip-top, at least superficially. Before too long, however, everything on my screen froze. I wasn't sure whether this was the machine just slowing down again, so I waited for a little while. There was still no joy. I attracted the attention of one of the staff, who were sitting around smoking and chatting.

"OK, OK, this machine please!" he said to me, gesturing that I ought to come and sit down at a PC across to my right. Somebody else came along and turned the first computer off, placing an improvised 'out of order' sign over it. I listened to the new console slowly cranking into action, clicked onto a couple of virtual buttons, and then the same thing happened again. I waited. Nothing was happening. I looked around at my fellow travellers, all with identical expressions of earnest concentration on their cathode-ray lit faces, and seemingly more patience than Harold Shipman. Again, I hailed the barman over.

"OK, this machine is working now" he told me, indicating the computer that I had just ten minutes previously forsaken, and removing the out of order sign. He beckoned me over to the still-warm swivel chair. "Over here."

As I was moving toward him he turned the CPU on and off a couple of times, and there were numerous bleeps and whorls of furious tinny sound as he attempted to bypass the automatic disc scanning and virus protection software. Finally, I found myself logging into one of my many Hotmail accounts and twiddling my thumbs as the tortuously slow connection attempted to run its course. I waited and waited as the other net-heads one by one drifted away to their beds, and I wondered whether I would ever get to mine.

The reason for this painful procedure lies not in the primitive nature of the computer equipment, which is any case absolutely fine, but instead with the outdated and poorly maintained standard of telecommunications infrastructure in so much of the West Bank. If you walk down any Palestinian city street and look above you, you will generally see telephone wires hanging in unprotected and uninsulated bunches at the top of their poles and across the street, and often held together with crocodile clips and the like[xxviii]. As a result of this, it was almost ninety minutes before I had managed to send out a grand total of four e-mails both to myself back at home and to the Hackney Gazette, my local newspaper. Although I was having to copy-type my notes from my journal[xxix], none of these were particularly lengthy, and this is really just another example of the lack of investment in Palestinian towns and cities that is both brought on, and then exacerbated, by Israel's general closure policy. It cannot be stressed enough that the closure system is primarily one of economic warfare being waged against the fledgling Palestinian Authority[xxx].

The next day began on time much as the one before, and we were given a half hour to get into our affinity groups before we were told of the schedule for the final day's training. Us tapdancers went through nominations for press officer, jail solidarity officer, medical officer, and decided who was arrestable and who non-arrestable. This was purely up to the individual. I decided to put myself forward as the press contact, as I enjoyed writing, although I had at that time no intention of composing so long a piece as this.

The main focus of the day, with the real action looming on the horizon of the next sunrise, was to be preparation for our very first action. We were going to get transport into Ramallah, where the PA president Yasser Arafat was being kept prisoner in his government compound by Israeli tanks and intermittent aerial assaults, and then sit down in front of one of those tanks in a silent protest, a "die-in". Although the tanks had largely withdrawn from the immediate vicinity of the compound, they were now occupying a nearby residential neighbourhood and holding it under almost total curfew. Although this was to be a measured and peaceful protest, and really little more than a press conference in the appropriate setting, the threat of danger would be all around us at all times. Only a few days beforehand, ISM internationals who had arrived in Palestine a week or so early had staged a similar event and had been subject to tear gas and sound bombs. It also turned out that, due to a banner that had been unfurled in that instance and draped over one of the compound's exterior walls (reading, "IT'S THE OCCUPATION, STUPID!"), president Arafat now wanted to meet with at least some of us, to thank us for our support at this particularly trying time. In view of the potential dangers of what would be, for many of us, our first experience of facing nervous teenage conscripts in control of real and dangerous armaments, the morning would be taken up by practising what is known as "60-second decision-making".

Rick and Leanne from CPT Hebron outlined the procedure. We would get back into our affinity groups and go through a given situation, with each individual stating their opinion in turn and responding to the those of the others, and a minute later we ought to have reached a consensus. In the interests of speed and efficiency, agreement could be shown by silent hand wiggling, a gesture which came to be known by all as "happy hands". After we had been practising this for a little while, the whole group would re-convene and then each affinity group would get up before the others, and then be taken through a further hypothetical situation to show that they had understood the procedure. Now, I've been through a number of meeting in my 36 years, and I am here to tell you that very few of them have been over in a minute! Nonetheless, the whole exercise went incredibly smoothly and I was left feeling remarkably empowered by the process. A fellow tapdancer, Trevor from outside of Seattle, who had been involved in the street protests against the WTO meetings held in that city in November-December 1999, told of how he had participated in an identical on-the-ground activity there. Only, in this case, it had involved 150 people sitting in the road at an intersection, and with heavily armed state troopers and chemical gas rapidly approaching. It hadn't been perfect, he said, it had taken a minute and a half, but it showed that it could be done. Some cold-hearted cynics among us said that we would wait and see about that, and we were proved wondrously wrong.

Following a slightly frustrating lunch-break where I found that the internet café had been closed for the day for maintenance work, we re-assembled at 2:30 to go through our final physical exercise, the practice die-in. Ghassan, Brian and Henry – possibly the West Bank's tallest man – again took on the role of angry IDF conscripts, with what I thought was a rather suspicious level of both gusto and insight into the workings of the military mind. The rest of us approached an imaginary tank and stood there in reverent silence for a moment before our pseudo-squaddies started shouting at us. It wasn't altogether easy for everybody to do this, even in the spacious dining hall with all of its furniture cleared away, and we had to take turns in sitting down in lines. "This is a closed military area! You are in danger!" Henry yelled at us in his best mid-western Israeli accent, and without all that much irony. "Please, you all have to leave now. You have one minute!" This was my first real grasping of what the morning's exercise might actually mean for me in a matter of only eighteen short hours. Henry picked up a plastic cup from the table behind him. I was getting scared. "This is a sound bomb!" he intimated to us in a whisper from behind his hand. Ghassan was marching up and down behind him with an invisible rifle clasped to his chest the whole time, pulling his best Judge Dredd face and hyperventilating loudly. Brian was standing off to one side, trying not to laugh. Henry threw the plastic cup into our midst. Thankfully nobody was injured, even when he screamed "bang!" at us maniacally. We had all had the foresight to cover our ears. Next there was another warning, followed by a tear gas grenade in the shape of a scrunched-up serviette. Then there came another. Soon it might be raining deadly hummus hankies and falafel crumbs. Most people pulled out their own bogus masks from their pockets at this point, steeped in virtual acetic acid, and covered their mouths. One or two elected to leave and stand at the sidelines, fearing the worst. Ghassan sprang into life, making a noise like a tank revving up its engine, a very accurate impression as I was to later discover. "Please move now!" Henry screamed at us again, before a few deserters left the front row of the symbolic sacrifice and the mock die-in had run its course.

As comical as this may sound, it was really quite a serious exercise, and a very useful one. I certainly felt a lot more confident about facing the might of the Israeli war machine than I had done a few hours earlier, when I had absolutely nothing with which to compare it. But, having said this, I was still rather petrified at the whole idea, preferring simply not to really think about it until almost the last moment. This tends to be just my way of dealing with any such situations. When I had told friends of my impending trip to the Holy Land, they had mostly asked me why I was going, with some bemusement. There's no easy answer to this, other than that you simply feel compelled to go. It isn't brave or heroic, and I was rarely in any direct danger. You go because you feel that you have to, or maybe just because you can. And whilst you're not exactly untouchable, you can at almost any point choose to just walk away. It's easy. We're privileged.

Our final briefing of the two-day session came from Allegra Pachecho, a solicitor of American extraction who is now an Israeli citizen, and who is dedicated in her human rights work with Palestinian civilians. She told us that she had first come to the West Bank after the signing of the Oslo accords, reasoning that now that there would be peace she could do her 'human rights year' in the new Palestinian state, and then return home to practice law there. Some six years later, she is still working in Palestine, still tirelessly daily grafting to get young Palestinians out of Israeli jails, of which she has had first-hand experience. She told us that if we were arrested in the days ahead, which was something that we all ought to expect, then our best course of action was to say nothing and sign nothing, and that we would all be released within a day, or maybe three, because of the embarrassment that Israel would face if it held internationals.

Later that evening, as I was preparing for an uneasy night's slumber with a last cigarette on my hotel balcony, Chris asked me:
"Alright there, Ted? You ready to sit down in front of a tank, then?"
"Yeah, I guess so," I told him.

The only way that I could finally justify it to myself and follow it through was to tell myself that it was too late to back out now; that I had made a minor commitment to a proud and beautiful people who are incrementally being 'ethnically cleansed' out of existence. And then, just for a second, I wasn't quite a tourist anymore.

Ramallah

We had an earlier wake-up than previously the next morning, as a coach was due to pick us up and take us towards Ramallah at 7:30am. I got all the coffee down that I could, but before I knew it Georgina was on her mobile calling the coach company: it was half an hour late already and there was still no sign. However, as it often is with these things, no sooner had her monologue begun to veer toward the slightly angry than she noticed it pulling up outside and she hung up, not quite apologising.

Everybody gathered up their extreme baggage collections and staggered outside, under their respective weights: it had been announced the previous evening that we would not be returning to Beit Sahour until December 23rd, some five nights away. From Ramallah we would be going on to Nablus, which is in the north of the West Bank, and it just wouldn't be practicable to journey back-and-forth to there from here, every day. It was stressed that we really ought to take along with us no more of our personal possessions than was absolutely necessary. Although this admonition didn't deter a few people from attempting to take all but the kitchen sink and a washer-dryer with them, I nonetheless felt a little justified in taking my entire belongings onto the bus with me. I really didn't know whether or not I would be coming back here, and I didn't have all that much anyway. Carrying a heavy bag through a few fields and up some muddy hill was the least of my worries.

An hour later we were approaching our first IDF military checkpoint, that which we had come through on our way in, at Bethlehem. Neta explained everything from the front of the bus, maintaining that should the soldiers get on board then we should let them, but under no circumstances ought we to explain to them that we were here to assist the Palestinian people in this, their darkest hour. For the purposes of this checkpoint we were tourists, on a trip.

The bus was waved to a stop, and three IDF soldiers approached as the driver pulled a lever to open the door for them. A captain got on and began speaking to Neta in English, asking her, "What is happening here?" She is of Canadian-Jewish extraction, and as such is very much the polyglot. Another soldier stood one step up onto the bus, peering inside at us, whilst the third hung around on the verge outside, looking up and down the road nervously. The second conscript generated a little curiosity and murmuring once we were on our way again, due the fact that he was clearly ethnically African, and therefore quite possibly not a direct descendant of Abraham and Sarah. Of course, it is now widely surmised that the Ashkenazi[xxxi] are in fact descended from the Turkic Khazar tribe, who converted to Judaism in the 8th century[xxxii], thus creating the first Jewish "state"[xxxiii] since the destruction of the second temple[xxxiv], but this is neither here nor there. Those black Israeli conscripts, of whom there are a highly visible number serving in the West Bank, are most likely to be either descended or grown up from Israel's spectacular airlifts of Ethiopian Jews, that is to say Operation Moses in 1994 and Operation Solomon in 1991. Indeed, Ethiopian Jews complain that are unfairly treated by Israel, often having to wait much longer for their free homes in the settlements than Russian immigrants; the anger of the Israeli-Ethiopian community exploded into riots two years ago when it was revealed that Israeli blood banks were secretly discarding their donations, fearing the blood might be tainted with AIDS.

After some explaining and head-nodding the captain turned to us, adjusted his shouldered automatic rifle slightly, and saluted.
"OK, have a nice trip!" he said to us, smiling. He got off and we were on our way. Neta had told him that we were tourists, on an outing to Ramallah for the day, and that had been that. They clearly hadn't been told about us as yet, and much like in the north of Ireland in the 1970s and 1980s, a policy of 'normalisation' seemed to be the order of the day. In a few days, however, a right-wing Israeli daily newspaper would be running a two-page spread on us, calling us 'the terrorist tourists'.

Before too long we were at our next checkpoint, to the north of Jerusalem. Here things would be a little different. Firstly, we had to gather up all of our possessions and leave the bus completely. It only had Palestinian registration plates, and as such it wasn't permitted to travel on the Jewish-only motorway, highway 60, that snakes north through Ramallah, Nablus, Jenin, and eventually all of the way up to Nazareth. We gathered up our things and went outside to retrieve our heavy back-packs and suitcases from the hold, if that's the right term, and then we began walking through the large set of obstacles as Palestinian civilians have to every day, simply in order to get to work, if they are allowed.

New concrete barricades had been put into place since Trevor and another tapdancer, Mika, had been here last, about two weeks beforehand. Whereas at that time the barriers had split the road into two lanes, now there were five, and increased security was all around. I looked up a steep embankment at barbed wire and ramshackle outhouses covered with tarpaulin, and I thought at first that this might perhaps be the edge of a Palestinian refugee camp, where three or four generations would have eked out their existences since the displacement from their homes in the 1948 war. Ever since the *Nakba*, the catastrophe, just surviving; then I saw the blue-and-white Israeli flag fluttering in the breeze, and I saw it for what it was. Another IDF position, raised up for easier surveillance of the many Palestinians who were daily just trying to go about their business, in their own country, under the occupation.

We moved to the side of the road and got into our Affinity Groups, in case of trouble from the army. Everything seemed to be relatively quiet, after a fashion, if you can discount the constant hubbub of voices and engine and truck horns; just the banal and dreary grind of another winter's morning under Israeli military rule. It's become ordinary.

We could have walked through the checkpoint along a separate channel, away from the harassment of Palestinians, we could have just flashed our passports and that would have been it. But that would have defeated the purpose of our being there. Even for those few 'fortunate' Palestinians who were born inside of the Green Line and have Israeli passports, and the number is decreasing even as their population increases due to the constant confiscations that go on at these concrete affronts to human dignity, even for these people the passport doesn't simply say 'Israeli citizen'. It says either 'Arab' or 'Jew'. So we stood in line with everybody else as documents were checked and double-checked. We refused to show our own passports out of principle, because we shouldn't have to and we didn't have to. I don't think that the soldiers really knew what to make of that.

There was another bus waiting for us at the other side of the checkpoint: another Palestinian bus, but this time with yellow plates. It took us speedily up Highway 60 to the outskirts of Ramallah, where we disembarked and prepared for a walk through the city centre. We could leave the bulk of our baggage behind this time though, as we were due to be picked by the same bus later and taken on a tour of the Salfit area, to the north. Because it was the rainy season, as I mentioned earlier, the proposed tree-planting action had been cancelled. Instead we would drive around the region with our guide, meeting ordinary Palestinian people and being shown the blockaded villages, and the settlements on nearby hilltops that were their cause.

Ramallah was teeming with activity on a Tuesday morning. Much like any middle-eastern town, there were the little souks, bakeries and food-stores everywhere, and we quickly found our way to a busy intersection where we were to meet a few representatives of the international press. There were Associated Press, Al-Jazeera, a promise from Phil reeves of the Independent, and a few others. Digital cameras were handed out to AG press contacts who didn't have them, and we were in no time walking past the bombed-out remains of The Voice Of Palestine radio station, formerly a BBC installation that had been set up by the British government in the 1940s. We paused here to get photographs. Huge billboard hoardings advertising Coca-Cola and Marlboro cigarettes were everywhere, a constant reminder of the cynical conditions of international aid that emanate from those who have stripped the poor of the world of their natural resources in the first place. We walked past Yasser Arafat's governancy compound, but there were no tanks evident, only the mess that they had left in their wake during the previous few weeks. Huwaida switched on her megaphone and the slogans began. "END THE OCCUPATION." "THE OCCUPATION KILLS." "NO JUSTICE, NO PEACE." The mood was upbeat as banners were unfurled and photographers ran ahead of the march to immortalise them. "You should bear in mind that snipers are active in this area, so everybody stick together!" Huwaida informed us. "Fuck's sake!" some wag replied, as the reality of the situation hammered home for the umpteenth time. And then we were at the edge of the besieged neighbourhood where our quarry lay, and where everybody is kept under constant curfew in their homes, and maybe allowed to go out and get food and supplies for an hour a day, if they're lucky[xxxv].

As it turned out, it wasn't a tank but an APC, an Armoured Personnel Carrier. Tommy informed us that these generally carry a crew of six men, with possibly a machine-gun post on the top. We stood in silence for about ten minutes as the APC's commander wondered just what to make of us. It moved forward a few yards, and then stopped again. The soldier sitting on the top made ready his rifle, and then he fired a live round into the air. Nobody moved. Then we all got down onto the ground for the die-in.

The die-in lasted for about twenty minutes. Some of the elderly had volunteered to sit in the front couple of rows, so as to deter any further movement from the APC, and it mostly stayed a short distance away. Huwaida utilised her megaphone to repeatedly emphasise that this was a peaceful protest, that the occupation is killing the Palestinian people, that it doesn't stop any of the violence but only makes it worse, and that peace can only be made possible once the occupation ends. All of this time Tommy was a tower of strength to his Affinity Group, the PSC[xxxvi]. He stood just to their left, calm and reassuring in his broad Brummie brogue, letting them know exactly what was going on in front of them, where their vision was impaired by their prone positions. "OK, there may be a concussion grenade in just a moment. When I give the word, I'd like to you all to just cover your ears. You'll hear a bit of a bang, that's all, just a bit of a bang." As it turned out, on this occasion the sound bomb never came, but his influence in keeping everybody – and not just those in his own affinity group – both calm and reassured, was widely considered to be invaluable.

We were due to have been laying down in the road for half an hour, but after 20 minutes had elapsed an elderly Palestinian gentleman came back from doing his shopping. As was explained to us later, he is somebody who lost an arm in the 1948 war, and who daily defies the curfew, almost daring the IDF soldiers to take a shot at him. He wandered into our midst and began lecturing to us on the occupation and the Intifada, in both English and Arabic. The more experienced activists elected at this point, in the interests of his safety, to cut the protest ever-so-slightly short, as the media interest had been capitalised upon, and our point had been made quite adequately by now.

As we walked back toward the governancy compound, all the talk was of Arafat. Was he merely a patsy for the illegal occupation that had been going on since 1967? Joan Beazleigh, a pensioner and tapdancer from south London who says that she has never been all that interested in 'issues' as such, was drawn to the injustice of the occupation and all of its connected issues when she let out a room in her house to a young man who had been born in Sabra camp.[xxxvii] His father had been taken away to be executed in the football stadium, but he too had miraculously managed to escape. Joan told me that Arafat had been a well-to-do civil engineer and a wealthy man, but that he had given all of this up to form Fatah[xxxviii]. Whilst I was not entirely convinced of his saintliness, I was impressed by this whilst recognising at the same time that, although he is almost all that the Palestinian people have at the moment, he has lost enormous ground in his seemingly-constant bending to the will of Washington. And Hamas[xxxix] is waiting in the wings.

As we reached the walls of the compound, a delegation of Palestinian Jerusalem businessmen were just leaving from their own audience with the great man. We were all ushered in with much efficiency, and following a five-minute trail through labyrinthine corridors, we found ourselves clustered round a conference table in a room that was clearly too small for the whole of our group, some 60-strong. After a little deliberation, we were relocated through a few more hallways to a larger room, and it was amusing to see the picture on the wall behind where the president would have been seated at the head of the table being taken down and transported with us.

Mr. Arafat duly appeared and worked the room, taking care to shake every last person by the hand as an entourage of enthusiastic photographers and a few bodyguards snaked along behind him at speed. He is a short fellow who now has trouble walking, which he does with the aid of a cane. He took his seat and gave a speech in perfect English, telling us how we were his people too, how grateful he was that we were here at this extremely difficult time, and that he loved us very much. There were a few questions and then the president apologised for his lack of hospitality, and said that he was arranging for some refreshments to be sent in. He reiterated that we were very welcome here in Palestine, and that we should stay and rest for as long as we wished, whilst availing ourselves of what turned out to be the generous array of comestibles on offer. I made a joke about how we ought not to stay for half a century as the Israelis had, but by this time he had gone on to business elsewhere. I then went into a total panic after discovering that my rented mobile phone and my collection of American dollars had apparently fallen out of my shirt pocket while

I had been laying down in the dirt in front of the APC, and I was much relieved to find out that they had all been recovered.

Our afternoon bus trip took us around the edges of the illegal settlement of Ariel, which is referred to elsewhere. As well as seeing all of the roadblocks that are essential to the closure policy for the first time, we also got our hands dirty when we helped to unload a truckfull of olive tree saplings across a roadblock in the rain, and were rewarded for our pains with the most delicious sweet black tea that I have ever tasted. We then journeyed through Jalazoun refugee camp via a servis, an entertaining experience. The roads around the camp, which is situated right next to an IDF base, have been blockaded and dug up to such an extent that any attempt to gain access resembles an admixture of scenes from Mad Max, rally driving and stock-car racing. After a couple of ditch-jumping contests and an assault up a 1:2 gradient, we came to rest on a slight plateau where a few children approached our vehicle curiously. Brian was in the front passenger seat and began conversing with one of them in his flawless Arabic. After the child had run back to join his friends, we asked him what they had been talking about.

"I asked him what he thought about the Israelis coming along and digging up all the roads around his home" he told us.
"What did he say?"
"He just said, Ah, the world is rotten!"

After a while, our servis took us out of the other side of the camp to our waiting bus. We got on, and were then taken on an extensive tour of the area around Ariel. We saw the many Israeli army outposts and checkpoints, not the large checkpoints but ad-hoc IDF adaptations of Palestinian bus shelters, fortified with arrangements of the kind of concrete blocks that had been used to separate the road into lanes at the major checkpoint we had walked through earlier.

Because of the blockade on farming, much food has to be bought from Israel at greatly inflated prices. The Palestinians experience great difficulty in transporting food because of all the roadblocks: these are usually piles of boulders and earth about 1.8 metres high, laid across the road. All food and other basic supplies have to be unloaded at the roadblock, and crates carried over by hand and then reloaded into another truck. This problem is compounded where the Israeli army places two or even three successive roadblocks on one road as a gratuitous extra punishment, and where food may have to be carried by hand between them for more than 100 metres.

Ambulances can't cross, and visits from medical teams to the beleaguered villages is only possible once a month, owing to the time taken to access them. The inhabitants are incapable of pursuing their jobs in nearby towns because it now takes them several hours to reach them through great detours, too long to be able to return the same day.

This is typical of villages all over the West Bank. We spoke to one taxi driver in the village of Yasuf, who tries to transport people from village to village. He says that he is always being stopped and given fines and tickets, "for being an Arab." Sometimes the army have ordered all of the people out of the taxi, and then burst his tyres. He told us that he had bought his taxi new, before the second Intifada, and that he's now obliged to repay the loan that he took out to pay for it. He should stay in his village, but he daily defies the siege and comes out to work. He told us that he doesn't care whether he lives or dies.

We drove past the huge Israeli industrial estates and chemical works - presumably where many of the residents of Ariel are employed – which are also situated on high ground, and which spill out their waste and detritus with reckless abandon into the Palestinians' natural water supply, leaving gullies of stinking effluent and black mulch where once were verdant streams. Later, we pulled over onto the side of the road so that a few of us could get out and investigate what at first appeared to be a sewage treatment facility for Ariel, which was clearly visible on the hill above. On closer inspection, however, it turned out to be nothing more than a badly fenced-in area where a waste pipe discharged all of the crap of the settlement into a previously pure and much-used Palestinian aquifer outlet, Wadi Kanaa. Walking around the edges of it, the stench was unbelievable even beneath the steady downpour of persistent drizzle. Mike from Michigan reassured us all that it wasn't anything chemically hazardous, that this was merely the stink that any rotting matter would give off; but there was a still greater stench behind this apparent thoughtlessness. Such wanton waste and destruction clearly betrays the real attitude of the Jewish settlers here: that the Palestinians are less than human[xl], that they don't matter, and that this mess can be cleared up after they have all been driven from their lands.

It was dark by the time that we reached our final destination for the day, an annex of Bir Zeit university. Here we would be meeting with students from the college and spending some quality time with them, as well as partaking in a veritable smorsgabord of delights to be brought in from a nearby restaurant, and being entertained by traditional Palestinian singing to the accompaniment of the *Bazouki*, a local musical instrument.

After I had been across the road in an internet café for about an hour, taking advantage of the speedy local connection I mentioned earlier, I found that the students had duly arrived and the food as well. We sat around in small groups, alternating between tables as they told us about how their university had been completely closed for three months, and that even if it reopened now they might have to re-take an entire year. Many of them were from Gaza, and they couldn't get the special passes needed since 1991 for access to Bir Zeit, so they had come illegally. As a result of this they couldn't take the risk of going back to visit their families, even then at the end of Ramadan, which is effectively "our Christmas", as one of them told me. Some had even not seen family members for some eighteen months, all this in spite of an undertaking signed by Israel and The PLO in 1995 granting a right of safe passage to and from Gaza.

I wandered into a packed adjoining room to check out the joyous singing and other sounds emanating from within. People wandered in and out, and I had just managed to secure a seat when the turn came for the visitors to sing something of their own. It was spontaneously decided, by whom I'm not sure, that a Bob Dylan rendition was in order. I had almost managed to sneak out unnoticed when some nasty grass from shoulder-to-shoulder grabbed a hold of the hem of my jumper, crying out that I couldn't leave now! I squirmed, made a break for it, and only just made it away from the hubbub in time. I was later informed that it had been hard, but it had to be done together. Leonard Cohen might have been more bearable. Ah, the world is rotten.

After many thank-you's and the polishing off of the cakes, we were driven away to our separate billets in some of the outlying villages. Most people were keen to get their heads down by this time, but myself and George Roussopoulos sat up late talking with our hosts, drinking a great deal of tea and smoking many cigarettes. We discussed at length the lack of freely-available information on the plight of the Palestinian people in the western hemisphere, particularly in the United States and Canada, and decided that much of this was down to the domination of the world's media by the former nation. George is a middle-aged Londoner and an active member of the PSC there, and I owe a great deal of the factual accuracy of this report to his assiduous note-taking. We also discussed the completely military nature of the history of the Israeli state, the Irgun and the Stern gang, Barak's foray into Lebanon dressed as a woman to liquidate a member of Black September, and Arafat's abandonment of the 1948 refugees. It was agreed that the parties to the Oslo accords could never hope to resolve the conflict, and the all-important land question, without explicit reference to this. At some point Brian and Sofia Ahmad, our organiser from Bir Zeit university and a US citizen of Palestinian parentage (she describes herself as 'Palestinian-American'), arrived with further supplies for our breakfast. Upon glancing at our watches, we agreed that we had better hit the sack immediately and the next thing that I knew it was 6:30 in the morning, and time for a whole new day.

The Media War

Inasmuch as I intend to make this chapter as brief as possible, I will try to use the space available here to explain the role of the independent media *as I see it* in the struggle for a free and independent Palestine. This hopefully will be done in the context of the wider attention afforded to the region in the mainstream media, with particular attention being paid to the power of video and still photography. Of course, it can very reasonably be argued that watching television is in and of itself a thoroughly alienating influence, and one that is detrimental to participation in any struggle, or to anything else for that matter; but that's another book.[xli] So I'll stick to the point and get this out of the way, then we can get back to the grassroots report, which is where it's really at.

For a long time here in The UK, there was a debate going on in radical circles over the presence of cameras on demonstration *per se*. I don't know where it stands at the moment, but there was a very healthy awareness of how any visual footage could easily be captured, taken out of context, and used against us. Imagine, for example, that you're taking a photograph – just a snapshot really, something to put on the wall at home, for your own amusement – of a group of people kicking in the window of McDonalds on New Oxford Street as the CARF demo marches past. Then a snatch squad goes in, and you're arrested too. You're charged with the offence of Violent Disorder, but this is later dropped to a bind-over for a year, which you reluctantly accept. However, those window-kickers have not been so lucky. Two of them were also nicked and they're looking at 10 years or more under the new terrorism act. The police now have your film and it constitutes, whilst not the whole case against them, at least a part of it. How would that make you feel? Or them?

While this is all mere hypothesising, there was the famous case just a few years ago of the alternative news video service 'Undercurrents'. They'd filmed a demonstration against the Criminal Justice Bill where there had been a little bit of unruly behaviour, and then the BBC came to them with an offer. Because they had no footage of the events in question, could they get some from Undercurrents? A fee of between 30 and 50 pounds was agreed, or so I believe, and the excerpt was shown on the national news, later to be handed over to the police for possible prosecution purposes.

If you need any more proof of the innate corruptibility of film as a medium, then look no further than the running battles between police and pickets at Orgreave during the great strike of 1984. Without warning, masses of riot police – and some British army disguised as such - charged the lines of pickets, only to be partly repelled in a hail of ad-hoc missiles, using (naturally) whatever lay to hand. The events were of course edited and then televised in reverse order the same day, thus giving the impression that the police were merely defending themselves against an unprovoked charge from masses of communist hooligans, and seeking to restore order. This whole obsession with seeing yourself or your friends either on the national news or in the 'proper' newspapers, is infantile in the extreme. It stems from the modern nonsense-culture of Big Brother and all the other forms of crass and objectionable 'reality TV', a term that is surely newspeak of the highest order. It's truly vacuous, a pissyass excuse for really being alive, and the ultimate concretization of the society of the spectacle. Getting on television is the same as watching television.

I'm going to contradict myself now, and say that in Palestine the situation is very different. A demonstration there not the same as a demonstration in Park Lane or Washington Square. Unless it's been organised by Peace Now or Gush Shalom then tear gas, sound grenades, rubber bullets and a damn good battering are guaranteed, with a strong likelihood for Palestinian participants of indefinite imprisonment and torture after a violent arrest: if they're lucky. Most people who demonstrate in Gaza and the West Bank have almost nothing to lose in doing so. So what might the role of international independent journalists and film-makers be in all of this?

My understanding of the purpose of our trip was that it was to be 50% geared to raising media awareness of the plight of the Palestinian people in their daily lives, with the other half of our work being practical assistance on the ground. This would take the form of removing IDF roadblocks in the affected areas (practically the whole of the West Bank), as well as checkpoint monitoring and such activities as the re-planting of trees on stolen Palestinian land. Checkpoint monitoring serves the dual purposes of both statistics-gathering and pure human witnessing, as well as that of deterrence: the proximity of cameras and press badges will hopefully minimise the brutality of the Israeli army, at least in the very short term.[xlii] There is also the matter of getting that information out. Everything is so thoroughly one-sided and upside-down in terms of media representation with regards to Palestine that very little of balance or value emerges. Israeli press agencies run a very tight ship, and most journalists do not seem that bothered about going beyond them to see things for themselves. So the CNN-BBC-IDF axis perpetuates the myth that Israel always acts in retaliation against the brutal and 'subhuman'[xliii] Arab terrorists, who only want to destroy Israel and kill all the Jews. For example, 'there has been an upsurge in violence recently with Palestinian suicide bombers attacking Israeli targets and the Israeli army responding with incursions inside Palestinian-controlled territories' reads a BBC online news item from as recently as February 1st of this year (2002). This was in an article purporting to be principally concerned with Ariel Sharon's flagrant disregard for the political process, following an interview he had given to the Israeli daily Maariv in which he stated he was only "sorry that we didn't liquidate him [Palestinian Authority president Yasser Arafat]" in Beirut in 1982. Such loaded comments pass almost without notice in the national press, and elsewhere, with regularity. The clear bias and obfuscation at work here beggars belief.

It would be very easy for Palestinians to hate all westerners based on the lies that are told daily about them. Walking through the mists of Jallazun refugee camp near Ramallah one filthy morning, where the rain and the mud were so severe that our group had to stop in order to reassemble almost every five or ten minutes, myself and a companion were accosted at a corner by a resident of the camp. "So who is the terrorist now?" he belaboured us in English. "Since 1948 we have been the terrorists! Who is the terrorist now?" I am ashamed to say that we could barely find an answer for him, although that answer is very clear. His desperation and potential for aggression were indeed palpable, and the two of us only stood there, almost speechless with grief and shame. Agreeing with him with all of our hearts, we just couldn't find the words.

But this media mendacity may all be changing. Numbered among our group, who had all paid for their own passage from their respective countries of residence, must have been around five professional reporters. I spoke to one, Alex Klaushofer, in the weeks after we had both returned to London. She's a London-based journalist who writes on politics and social affairs for various publications, including the monthly magazine of the independent left, 'RED PEPPER'.

"I have a long-standing interest in the Palestinian cause" she told me, "and I wanted both to see what was going on, and to show support at this particularly difficult time. As a journalist, I felt the best way I could do this was to go and get some coverage of the current situation. I certainly didn't make any money from it - it cost me money – but I felt that as a journalist, and as a supporter, it was worthwhile."

Independent media representation of the Palestinian struggle for a just peace, and human rights and freedom, is absolutely essential. Although Samaritan acts of beauty and kindness in the occupied territories are of course at least equally as valuable, in the long haul the battle will only be won by bringing the truth of the situation on the ground to the eyes of the world. I would urge every right-minded journalist and film-maker to contact the ISM, and to get out there for the time of the next mass actions. Palestine needs you.

Salfit

Although I will refer back to the Salfit region a number of times in the course of this book, I really feel that it merits a chapter all its own, as it was the place where I spent most of my worthwhile time in Palestine. This involved helping to dismantle a few of the IDF roadblocks that form the bulwark of the Israeli closure system. It was also to be, for me, where I met with much of the warmth of the Palestinian people, and also where we were all confronted almost daily with a measure of their unassailable grief.

A servis picked us up from our accommodation shortly after breakfast at 7am, and following a brief road journey through the mist and rain, we were once again negotiating the muddy terrain of Jalazoun camp. On this morning the camp really was the archetypal embodiment of third-world poverty, exploitation and disinvestment. It is a constant source of amazement to me, a self-confessed scruffbag, how the vast majority of Palestinians maintain their immaculate appearance under such insufferable conditions.

We left the van and met with the rest of our group. We would now have to carry our heavy packs over the potentially treacherous debris and boulders, through the slippery mud and rubble, as many of Jalazoun's residents have to daily to get to work or school. There is single UNHCR school at Jalazoun, one of the few in the West Bank that has managed to stay open pretty much daily throughout this Intifada. It was agreed to make our way on to the first road crossing at a steady pace, where we would temporarily regroup. Needless to say, there was much confusion in the fog and the murk, and our procession quickly became strung-out and fragmented, with some of the more athletic venturing too far ahead and becoming lost in the soup. Those who had stopped at the road reconvened, and it was agreed that George would head up our trek to stop the over-enthusiastic from getting too far ahead, with Angie positioned at the back to watch out for stragglers.

Eventually we did all reassemble at a rudimentary taxi rank close to the school, and a number of these were ordered to take us back into Ramallah, which was as far as they said that they could go. Salfit itself is the general hub of the area. Boasting a population of about 10,000, it should provide the centre for all of the essential services in the locality, which is comprised of a number of surrounding satellite villages. It had been completely closed for five days prior to our visit, when IDF special forces had dramatically and without warning re-entered the town, killing six people. One of these was murdered in front of his wife and children, and another had been shot before an APC drove over his head, making his body unrecognisable. The closure of Salfit means that all of the neighbouring villages are completely cut off from the services which should emanate from it, particularly the fire service, the hospital situated there, and the Palestinian Red Crescent ambulances that provide for it.

Jawad Abd Ellatif Abd Elraheem Dimms was a native of Salfit, who fell to an Israeli soldier's bullet during the attacks on December 14th 2001. At around 2:30am, he heard the approach of the Israeli special forces and he ran to his friend's house to warn him: although he himself was not on any Israeli 'wanted list', it seems that his friend may have been. As he was knocking on the door, IDF soldiers shouted at him to stop and then shot him in the chest. He was 26 years old, and a graduate in Education and Psychology who had been unable to find work because of the closure policy. He had been married for five months. His mother said, *"They didn't have the guts to confront us with their tanks and guns, so they cut off the power before they came in."*

We were invited into the home of Jawad's parents to share in their grief. The women filed into the closed area of the kitchen to hear from his widow, whilst the men sat around on chairs that had been brought into the main room of the house for this period of *Aaza*, a paying of respects which lasts for about a month. The dead man's father sat in the middle of the room and related to us again an account of how Jawad had fallen, and his grief became increasingly tangible in its intensity: our guide was present, and he translated for us. Here was a thoroughly broken man, a man who could barely lift his head, whose eyes were flushed red raw from all the days and nights of wailing and tears. What can I do, he was asking us. How can I go on now? He was my son, my only son, he was everything to me and now I have nothing. We couldn't answer him. Although some questions were asked before we left, our silence was palpable and you could have cut the atmosphere with a knife. There was simply nothing for us to say. This was surely the occupation in microcosm.

Cups of bitter coffee were passed around during our meeting: this is also traditional during the mourning period. When a respectful amount of time had elapsed and it seemed that there was nothing left to say, we got up to leave and I managed to commit another atrocious faux pas. In my embarrassment I stumbled, and when my size elevens came to rest it was with a splintering crunch on top of two or three of the ornate coffee cups. Back on the bus, Huwaida assured everybody that the belief here is that when something is broken, it's not necessarily seen as a bad thing. Rather, she said unconvincingly, you are breaking a greater evil, which translates as meaning that you are using up some of the evil around you, and thus preventing a bigger tragedy from occurring in the near future. Curiously, I didn't feel any the better for it.

We also visited a small emergency clinic, one that was originally developed in order to tend to those serious medical emergency cases who are unable to get past the checkpoints to larger hospitals since this Intifada began. It's of particular use for women who are going into labour, and due to the closures it now takes at least three hours for residents of the outlying villages to reach a hospital. We spoke with Dr. Naiem Sabra, the director and the surgeon at the hospital, which has a grand total of five doctors and four beds. It serves 60,000 people in the Salfit area, as well as a large part of the population of nearby north Nablus.

Issa Naif Souf is in his mid-thirties, married, and the father of one child; he is now paralysed from the waist down. Several months previous to our visit he was at his home in one of Salfit's satellite villages. His brother's children were playing in the olive fields near their home when Issa heard that soldiers were approaching, throwing tear gas grenades. Issa ran out to bring the children in. Two of them came back, and he was shouting for the third, when the soldiers opened up with automatic fire. A bullet passed through one of his lungs and shattered when it reached his spinal column. As he fell the soldiers ran up and began kicking him, shouting: 'Get up! Get up!' He tried to stand up again, but by now he could feel no sensation in his legs; he shouted for his friends. When one of them appeared, a soldier pointed his gun at him. His last recollection is of begging the soldier 'to be human' before he lost consciousness. When he woke, a doctor told him that he would be permanently paralysed. He still has nine pieces of the bullet lodged in his spine. Issa was formerly a sports instructor.

During a stop at Kefl Haris, we had been cordially invited to stay for our three days of non-violent direct activism in the region, in three houses in the village of Marda. Marda is a traditional village, so we were billeted separately, with all of the men stationed in rooms upstairs in what appeared to be the village social club, and the women spread over two residential homes. The ISM had money set aside for our accommodation in local hotels and hostels, and this was given to the villagers who used it to feed us far more than adequately. Other than our obvious desire to be with the Palestinian people as much as was possible, it's also considered very offensive in the local culture to refuse hospitality. This was a fact of which I was later informed, as we worked away at the roadblocks through squally and freezing showers, buzzing away merrily on the caffeine from their delicious coffee. Whilst I can't speak for the women, in our own lodgings there was no hot water for washing, nor heat for drying our sodden clothes. This was exacerbated by the fact that the doors of the downstairs hall were more often than not thrown open to the night, as it was where our endless debriefings and planning meetings for the next day's activities were held. Also, our very presence seemed to attract the attention of almost the entire neighbourhood. As this was how honoured guests – as we most clearly were – were treated, I dread to think what conditions must have been like, day to day, for the ordinary villagers of Marda.

We were dropped off just outside the village of Yasuf at around 9am, where we found that there were indeed two roadblocks, spaced about 100 metres apart. We split ourselves into two groups, and after a brief interval some of the villagers came out carrying tools such as small shovels, pickaxes and plastic buckets. These were for the time being for our use only, but as the day passed without much harassment from Israelis, some of the burlier examples of the fruit of Palestinian manhood joined in, putting most of our own efforts to shame. We began by digging away the earth at the top of the barricade, in an attempt to locate the huge concrete blocks - impossible to dislodge without the aid of a bulldozer - that surely lay concealed within. This done, we were able to then position a space wide enough for a vehicle to pass through, at one side of the impasse, and shovel away. It's therefore unnecessary to waste one's time clearing away the whole of the obstruction, and the earth doesn't even have to be completely flattened, only basically negotiable for a car or a van. During the course of the day the sky alternated between a sharp and beautiful blue, and dark angry bulkheads of cloud from which we were frequently showered with torrents of freezing rain. From time to time a pickup truck from the nearby settlement, equipped with overhead searchlights, would appear on the brow of the hill and linger for a while. Brian informed this that this was not even the Israeli police but 'settler security', and told us not to worry about it. The truck would then drive away, and wend its way back and forth along the road above, as if under orders from some higher power to let us alone for the time being. It returned to observe us several times throughout the day.

My own labours began ignominiously, as I bestrode the roadblock like a moderately overweight Behemoth and began funnelling scatterings of mud onto the side of the road, thus obscuring the track that Yasuf's pedestrians had been using to access their village. After having cleared up the mess I had made, I took instead to standing at the bottom and heaving away any boulders that were sent tumbling down by our more astute volunteers. We worked on through the wind, rain, and often slippery mud for three or four hours, until a passing space had finally been cleared. By this time, a small crowd had gathered and the first vehicle – after a few mishaps with the mud – was able to get through, amid much jubilation and cheering. As the other roadblock was still being levelled, the IDF arrived and began to question those at work there. A chain was formed across the front of the roadblock to engage with the soldiers, while the work carried on behind it. After Hanna had conversed with them in Hebrew for a little while, they went away again.

Back at Kefl Haris, which is close to Ariel's petrol station, settlers had been slowing down as they drove past to wind down their windows and hurl abuse. Both the army and settlement police were already present and work was going on when, suddenly, two enormous settlers emerged from around a corner and ran at the activists, yelling abuse, and generally lashing out in all directions. They were, however, quickly arrested[xliv].

 We found this out when Brian had finally got onto the other team on his mobile phone to see what was going on there: the main transport was with them, and so we had to wait. What was also happening at the other end was that the bus driver had been forced off the road by a pair of IDF jeeps, hemmed in, fined for parking there illegally, and given points on his license. Eventually we were able to continue back to Marda, where an enormous spicy supper was waiting for us almost as soon as we had got our filthy boots off and walked in the door. And as soon as we had got that and some more coffee down, then the meetings began.

"OK" Neta started. "We were originally going to suggest that tomorrow, we can either go back to the villages for more roadblock removals, or we can go and do roadblock removals at a couple of the other villages, *or* we can do what we call a 'peace ride'. A peace ride is where we take our bus onto the settler-only highway, we park we bus and we block the road for an hour or so. However, our bus driver quit. That's his prerogative, and I for one don't blame him!"

Our options were therefore narrowed down to whether we went back to the same places or descended upon somewhere new. A representative of the local population briefed us on their views with regard to this. He said that we should not worry that Yasuf, Marda, Hares, or anywhere else might suffer reprisals because of our activities. He said that the villagers all over were saying that they are suffering anyway, that things cannot possibly get any worse for them, and that they want us back. We were both honoured and relieved by this, of course, but it nonetheless remained a constant concern.

Roadblock removal on the following day followed, for the group that I was with at least, much the same successful pattern as before. The army cruised by on occasion, eventually pulling over to speak with us and even wishing us 'a nice trip'; only one settler vehicle stopped, its occupant asking us to take down a banner saying 'End the occupation'. We refused. "You ought not to trust the Arabs, they are wild people, it says so in the Bible!" this man who bore more than a passing resemblance to the goat that he kept in the back of his truck informed us. However, the other team appeared to be jinxed, unless of course my cup-smashing ritual had not gone unanswered by one of the Holy Land's many deities. Having returned to the site of the previous day's assault to keep open their handiwork, they then had to deal with the police, the army and an IDF Caterpillar bulldozer. Just as it seemed that all was lost, Sofia Ahmad of Bir Zeit University had run out in front of the offending plant machinery, screaming away to her heart's content. The result for her was a few hours spent in the police station inside Ariel settlement, and a few very muddy Israeli policemen.

Meanwhile, the bus had been delayed again, Marda had been declared a closed military area, and as a consequence we had all been invited to stay the night in Hares. We had just about finalised a schedule for staying up overnight to keep an eye on the open roadblock, when Marda was just as suddenly opened up once more and we started to return there in shuttle runs of ten people at a time. We had withdrawn to a house in the village for coffee and treats, and where a brazier had been lit out on the veranda for the hardier people to stand around, while the rest of us amused ourselves on the comfortable sofas and chairs within. Our main concern at this time was Joan, who has a condition whereby she reacts severely to any sudden drop in temperature by appearing to go into shock. It ostensibly resembles hypothermia, and even if it isn't, it's clearly still a very dangerous thing. Joan was losing all sense of her extremities: we were very glad to get her out of there, and immediately made contingency plans for future scenarios so that this wouldn't happen again.

Some of our number had been annoyed at having to leave the village at all, having promised our hosts that we would be there to keep their roadblock open overnight. This, as was mentioned previously, might well be considered disrespectful. Then the news reached the meeting-house in Marda that the IDF had re-sealed the village that we had just abandoned. They did this in a particularly demeaning manner, by stopping a passing Palestinian motorist and forcing him to drive onto the passing point of one of the cleared roadblocks before confiscating his keys and forcing him to abandon his vehicle, and thereby blocking access into the village at the same time as potentially depriving a family of its livelihood. Four or five ISM activists – including the tapdancers Angie and Rachel – took it upon themselves to rectify the situation. They made their way back there, tracked down the army patrol responsible and demanded back the man's car keys. After a brief exchange of views the keys were handed over, returned to their rightful owner, and the village became once more accessible. It remained so for more than 48 hours, and our stalwarts returned to Marda in plenty of time for that evening's extensive planning meeting.

The meeting itself was a long and fractious one, where the beginnings of some kind of a schism seemed almost to be developing. The roots of the only real disagreement of our campaign lay in an action that had been proposed for the following day. Several of us had decided that it would be a spectacular media exercise to again waylay an Israeli tank, this time one that was blocking access into the city of Nablus. The tanks in question were positioned on the main road near to the Palestinian village of Tel, on a hilly pass leading out toward the Salfit region. We wanted to approach the tank, coax it off the road if at all possible, and then in some way affix slogans to its side. The most popular mode of decoration for those proposing this action seemed to come in the form of brightly-coloured paint. A number of people regarded this as tantamount to vandalism, and other possible ways of achieving the same ends were suggested and then thrashed out throughout the evening, all to no avail. The main obstacle for the proposers was that, under the whole group's understanding of the consensus system, just one vote of dissent – albeit one that should be grounded in a firm moral objection – amounted to an effective veto. There were frayed nerves on all sides, and it was eventually decided that the best thing would be for us all to go to bed and then continue in the morning, when we would all hopefully be feeling a little refreshed. Either way, we were going to Nablus to meet with the city governor.

Nablus

As it turned out, a compromise proposal had been thrashed out by members of 'shoulder to shoulder' and a couple of other individuals after everyone else had retired for the night, one that was surprisingly amenable to all. Under this new proposal those who wanted to participate in the action could do so, whilst anybody who still felt uncomfortable with it would go slightly on ahead to form an observation party. The action would now involve the affixing of our slogan, plus a poster of one of the Palestinian martyrs[xlv] from Nablus - whose bereaved family and mourners we were scheduled to visit earlier in the day - to the side of the tank. If this proved impracticable, then those who were prepared to do so would sit down in the road in front of it. It was also agreed that the action would only take place after our visit to the town, on the way back out toward Beit Sahour, and then only if there was still time.

We again journeyed by bus as far as we could, before reaching a roadblock from where we had to walk a short distance. Although it was a gloriously sunny day many activists were now falling prey to a minor flu epidemic, the result of three days spent in the cold and rain of greater Salfit. The road to Nablus is almost akin to a mountain pass, and the scenes are that which you might expect to see on 'Newsnight' or somesuch, of any international refugee situation. There were crowds milling around, servis taxis standing by on the lookout for business, a cacophony of horns a-beeping, and donkey carts filled with local produce in abundance. Responsible individuals were nominated to ensure that none of us became lost in the milieu this time, and only once were the rear guard almost left behind themselves. I say this with confidence because that rear guard were Joe Button And myself. We were just hurrying the last of our group along when we were approached by a couple of locals who clearly only wanted a chat on this beautiful day, asking us where we were from.

"Sorry," we explained to him. "We're getting left behind here, and we have to go and catch up with our friends now or we'll be late!" "Why do you run from us?" he entreated, obviously both offended and hurt by our rudeness and apparent haste to get away. "We are not animals! We are human beings, just like you! Why are you afraid?" Of course, we had a very busy schedule to keep to, but once again I felt more than a little bit awkward and ashamed.

A short distance along the road, which overlooks terraced agricultural hillsides that are strongly reminiscent of Tuscany, we came to a second taxi rank and regrouped to arrange ourselves into groups of seven or eight. This is the average servis capacity. A local entrepreneur wandered about among us, clanging at the side of his steaming coffee pot with an ornately bejewelled teaspoon, and his wares proved simply too much for myself and Trevor to resist. There were cries from the front of "no photographs here, please!" as we neared our pick-up point, and this was unanimously respected. We waited around above the road in our affinity groups as we were packed into several of the constantly arriving and departing taxis, mostly one whole group at a time. Beyond where we were waiting there was a dry-stone wall, some scrub bushes and a few goats grazing: this all provided a very handy cover for three or four of us as the coffee began to do its stuff. "Gents to the left, ladies to the right!" some wag suggested.

On our way to the offices of the Nablus governancy we passed the bombed-out remains of a PA police station, where twelve local policemen had recently lost their lives. We also visited the remains of a small warehouse that had previously been storing furniture, waiting for the offices of the new authority to be completed. The remains of desks, swivel chairs, and filing cabinets lay scattered all around. Israel had described this facility as a "mortar factory", and it had been hit with two missiles from American F-16 fighter jets. Now little remained of it except for an enormous crater, some grotesquely mangled wreckage and quite a few piles of rubble. We journeyed on to the governor's office, where we were once again graciously received. This time we were all able to fit around a single conference table in one of the reception rooms. We were also provided with refreshing soft drinks, and even a number of microphones for the brief question-and-answer session that was to follow.

The governor was introduced by an official translator, who said that he probably wouldn't be needed as the governor could speak English very well by himself. As with President Arafat, this proved to be very much the case. Nablus had been completely sealed and declared a closed military zone a few days before our arrival, and the translator explained that this had been happening on and off for well over a year. Then the governor stood up to address us to a polite round of applause.

"Welcome," he began. "We hold your visit in very high regard. Our people all over Palestine are very aware of your presence here and appreciate it. It's so important for you to understand and convey what you see here and the effect it has on every Palestinian man, woman and child. Our people feel isolated and see the one-sided policy of the United States and other foreign governments. It is good to see that people - civilians - do not share their governments' views.
[We hold out to you] all of our appreciation for your help, in this struggle for peace. We, the Palestinian people, have chosen peace. Despite everything we see in our daily lives – the tanks, the suffering, the constant obstacles – we still seek peace. [But] peace must be based on justice from both sides.

We don't know how to achieve this peace when such one-sided policies are imposed. It is obvious to me that the government of Sharon does not see the Palestinians as human beings or as having rights to be respected. We see this by the actions of the Sharon government: land confiscations, settlements, closing roads, not allowing us to continue with our lives.

It's obvious that it's not only the daily killing of civilians, Sharon is also trying to kill our hope and our ideas – our mental struggle. The Sharon policies have killed off even contact between the two peoples. All the initiatives of peace have been demolished. The policies have taken us back many years.

I don't need to go into detail about the difficulties – I am sure you have seen this every day. All of our towns and villages are sealed off from each other.

Economically, workers cannot get between home and work, nor materials to factories. Farmers can't get to their land. Many farmers have been killed by settlers for trying to get to their land, and fields of crops burned. Nablus area has some very fertile lands, but we can't get to them, nor transport the produce. All this pressure is leading to economic starvation.

Looking at education, roadblocks stop students and teachers getting to places of study – such as the large university in Nablus. Teachers cannot get to the villages. The path you walked today, tens of teachers try to pass every day but are exposed to the brutality of soldiers. Some have been killed. Nearby villages have had no education for three months.

As for health, people who need medical attention cannot get from villages to Nablus – even when hurt for example by being shot by Israeli soldiers. Several Palestinian citizens have died at checkpoints when held up with medical conditions. I know at least two personally. Pregnant women have died, miscarried or delivered at checkpoints. These Israeli policies have affected every aspect of our daily lives. A small village fifteen kilometres from here has a spring which is often contaminated by nearby settlers. But this is the reality of siege and Israeli occupation. We are working to survive it, including with people from [the] outside.

We really don't see any way out of the situation we're currently in with someone like Sharon in power. What we need is people of good heart to stand up against this injustice, against their own governments which are supporting Israel. For we are being killed every day by the Israeli military and settlers, but the USA is providing them with tanks and guns. So we want good people like you to stand together and speak out. Thank you."

He sat down again to further applause, and then there was the opportunity for some questions from the audience, so to speak. Neta outlined the ISM's position to the governor, explaining how long we were staying in Palestine *en masse*, outlining what else we would be doing during that time, and pledging our heartfelt solidarity and support for the Palestinian people. Then Liz from Stamford Hill had a go.

"It's all very well our being here for a fortnight," she said, "temporarily dismantling a few of the roadblocks at Palestinian villages that are affected by the closures; helping with Olive tree planting; and staging symbolic die-ins in front of the Israeli tanks in those neighbourhoods under curfew. But at the end of those two weeks, we still have to go home. So what we want to know from you is, where else can we put on pressure to help you, particularly at this very difficult time, after we have gone from your country?"

The governor leant into his microphone.

"Everything we do is for the good," he said, "and we should always keep moving forward. A few months ago the United States looked very critical of Israel; not it appears to be much less so. But we should all realise, after September 11th, the effects of US foreign policy. There can also be efforts made to assert economic pressure on the Israeli state. The settlers poison the water and they kill us when we try to get to our land. We live with death and destruction daily. Everyone in Palestine has seen, and appreciates, your presence here – both through local media and through other sources. You can put pressure on your own governments too; this is very important."

After our audience with the governor, we all filed outside again where our bus was waiting for us. We stood around in the sunshine for a few more minutes, some of us smoking cigarettes while others discussed the most effective remedies that were available for the relief of the common cold. Whilst we had all enjoyed and possibly even benefited from this cursory exchange of views, what many of us were keen to get on to was actually meeting with the families and friends of some of Nablus' most recent martyrs of the occupation. This was to prove a much more difficult, and in some cases an absolutely gut-wrenching experience.

Deib Assad Abdul Hadi Alsarawi was murdered by the IDF on Thursday, December 20th – less than three days prior to our visit. Our tour guide explained to us that he had initially arrived home, happy because he had learned that the Israeli forces had pulled out of his town earlier that day. Suddenly he heard shooting, and he went out onto his terrace to see what was happening. As he appeared there, he was shot three times in the head and shoulders. His wife, who was at the time nine months pregnant, ran upstairs to find him and starting screaming for her neighbours: by the time that they arrived he was already dead. His wife also has shrapnel wounds in her wrist, neck and stomach, but she couldn't be operated on until after the delivery of their baby. The women of the family were needless to say grief-stricken, particularly due to the double-whammy of not only having lost their husband, son and brother, but additionally of seeing it reported on Israeli television as the shooting of a "Palestinian terrorist" who was "planning an attack".

We visited the Aaza, which was being held away from the family home in Nablus, in actual fact just across the street from yet another PA police station that had been partially demolished by Israeli military forces. We shook hands with the mourners and then we sat in reverent silence, as our guide outlined for us the circumstances of what he kept referring to as "the accident"; this was quite obviously a rather unfortunate mistranslation from whatever the Arabic might be for "the terrible event". Perhaps 'Nakba' would have been more appropriate[xlvi].

As it turned out, the family home itself was situated but a few streets away, just up the hill. We had been invited to present our condolences there as well, so many of us strode with as much decorum as we could muster out from the initial Aaza residence. We then had to go past the PA escort that was waiting for us outside and up a few flights of stone steps, to where Deib's widow, his sister and the other womenfolk of the household were gathering on their shaded terrace. This was to prove an altogether more exacting affair for all concerned.

Deib's window began to speak to us whilst choking back her tears, while Huwaida, Hanna and Diane Sellick – a British national who lives in Jordan, where she teaches English - attempted to translate. Even if you were unable to see her tear-stained cheeks and bloodshot eyes, you would have been quite easily able to guess - just from the timbre of her strained and shattered voice - that here was a woman who hadn't slept a wink since the tragic death of her young husband. She went over the facts of his brutal execution for us once more, and a few well-meaning individuals murmured to her that once they returned home they would tell everybody that they knew, all about it. That they would alert the international press, and petition their respective governments as to the sheer barbarity and the true nature of the occupation. In retrospect, this was entirely the wrong thing to say at the time given the circumstances, and the sheer recent proximity of events. This poor woman then launched into a grief-stricken tirade on our powerlessness, our meaninglessness to her, and even our own culpability as citizens of countries that are clearly the beneficiaries of the rule of force in world affairs.

"What can you do?" she beseeched us. "What can you do for us? You can do nothing for us! Every day they are doing this to us. Every day they are killing us, and still the world doesn't listen. And why? Why is this? Because the world doesn't care about us. Because nobody cares about us! And so, there is nothing that you can do for us – because nobody cares about us. Nobody cares whether we live or we die!"

There was indeed nothing more that could be said, and it was in a very sombre mood that we arrived to check into our luxury hotel in downtown Nablus. This took a lot longer than I was personally comfortable with, as there was a mandatory passport check required by the mostly toothless Nablus governancy. There was also the simple matter of sorting out who was sharing rooms with whom, and I didn't have the patience for it. I didn't really care who was going to be farting and snoring alongside me for a few short hours that night, I only wanted somewhere that I could put down my bags and my world-weary limbs for a short time, and just be alone with my thoughts. My temper had become shortened and very much frayed by the day's events, and I felt that I needed to be completely alone to thrash things out in my head before I could even attempt to speak in a reasonable manner to another human being. Of course, this must be what a great many Palestinians feel like every single day of their lives – and far worse – and they deal with it impeccably. It could be, of course, that they have a culture that precludes them from showing such feelings in public, but somehow I don't think so. I think it's more matter of their being much less selfish, and really much better mortals than I could ever hope to be. My week in Palestine was drawing to a close but a whole lot of soul-searching as to what kind of a person I was, and what kind of a world I really wanted to live in, was to follow. And of course, this isn't over.

Other people were anxious to get out and about of course, not least because of our own self-imposed curfew. In view of the situation, the ISM had decided that it would be unwise for any of us to venture outside of the hotel much after dark, at least not in smaller groups and without the help of a local or an experienced chaperone. Tommy and a few other people had checked in quickly and then ventured outside to catch the last hour or so of daylight, driven by a desire to see the flourishing *souk*. Some even went out to look for the local equivalent of a hardware store, in search of spectacularly coloured paint for the next day's activity, in spite of our agreed programme. But most of the rest of us took it much more steadily, indulging ourselves in long showers after our time in Marda, and in even longer periods of introspection. For some there were the delayed phone calls home, whilst I spent most of my time simply looking out of the window whilst knocking back copious amounts of decent coffee, which was possibly not such a good idea considering my mood. Eventually we got around to attempting a tapdancers affinity group meeting over a fifty-Shekel dinner, but nothing much really came out of it. Trevor echoed my own mood, saying that he couldn't really be around other people right now. I declined the hotel's kind offer of sitting through another screening of 'Shakespeare in love' and instead found an accomplice in Jordan for a sortie out to the local internet café, which was situated a short distance from the hotel. There was no gunfire, no running battles or kidnap attempts, and less than an hour later we made our way back to our beds via the hotel bar, where Tommy, Trevor, Mike from Michigan and a number of the locals were helping Saleyha to celebrate her birthday. Things began to get a little bit lively, with the Palestinian men taking turns to serenade her, but the atmosphere was still very much laid back and one of camaraderie. Finally, Jordan leant into my ear.

"I'm going to split," he told me, "before this turns into 'The Accused'!"

We bade our good comrades goodnight, and I was straight out the door alongside him.

*****

Tank-chasing is a blast: you ought to try it. Our quarry was blocking the road into Nablus as we walked out towards Tel. And so it was that we immediately came to the real business of attaching our slogan to its side: "RETURN TO $ENDER". As we approached the Merkava it drew back across to the side of the road, puffing out its acrid black diesel smoke. If we could just keep it there for ten minutes, we thought that a couple of taxis might be able to get into town for a while.

Feeling unable to shoot live ammunition or tank shells at internationals, the crew began to swing its barrel wildly from side to side as the message was pasted on. Part of the improvised writing blew off in the gusts of wind that were generated by the tank's sudden bursts of activity, and it was left up to Chris and Mike to bravely duck under the swinging gun turret with paper and paste. After several attempts, phase one was complete. It manoeuvred sideways, then back up the road, and there followed an hilarious scene where it appeared that unarmed peace activists were chasing a tank away from the vicinity of Nablus and Tel. A poster of Diab Sarawi, the martyr killed by tank fire two days previously, joined the decorations. Taxis and ambulances were thus able to get into town as the monster from Washington retreated from view to clean up. They honked their horns and waved at us in their delight as they drove past where we had the beast quarantined, and on into the city. This was a far better result than any of us had expected. We had opened the road into town, which hadn't even been a stated part of our objective, and nobody had even had to sit on the ground in front of the tank. At the last moment, an IDF jeep roared up to us from the direction of our observation party, at speed. But there was nothing to be done. The captain of the jeep got out to speak to us momentarily, but reporters from Associated Press were present, and they decided that they would leave it this time. This was a level of consideration that they wouldn't be showing for very much longer, if reports are to be believed[xlvii]. As we walked on down the hill to a round of applause from our observation party, we looked back to see the tank returning. And unfortunately there was nothing more that *we* could do here today: but we had more than made our point this time, and the roads can get very perilous for Palestinian bus drivers in the Nablus-Salfit region after sunset. We had to hurry. As we walked back to our waiting servis taxis, Israeli conscripts manning an APC asked us whether we had any American cigarettes for them. Tomorrow it would be Christmas Eve.

Leaving…

I was a bit scared, walking through Bethlehem checkpoint – alone - at three in the morning on Xmas eve. This was exacerbated by my taxi fare problems. We had agreed a price of forty Shekels for the short trip, which is about three times what it costs during the daytime. Fair enough. These guys don't have any money with the blockade - they don't have any anyway - and then they have to stay awake until this kind of an ungodly hour, just to do one pissy little job. I don't need the Shekels anyway; I'm going home. As I say, fair enough. Then the confusion starts. First, two guys arrive in the taxi. At first I assume that this is for safety reasons, but then when I ask he tells me that's not so. 'No, it's OK' he says, in what has become a familiar refrain around here. About half way to the checkpoint, we stop. I get out of the back and sit in the front. I notice that the driver's window is held in place with a screwdriver. The man who was driving goes into a house and his friend takes over. We carry on. This is the problem: it's no longer his cab. We agreed fifty, not forty Shekels, he says. But now we are facing the checkpoint and he can't get him on his mobile and it's not his cab. I only have 35 in change, plus a hundred note, and he has no change at all. All the time I am noticing the two Israeli squaddies glancing around at us, appearing to get increasingly nervous. There's a Palestinian car facing them with one door open and two people inside, chatting away conspiratorially (that's us). Finally I let it go, get out of the car, and begin to walk through. They come towards me with due deliberation as I realise that I'm clutching my day-pack in front of me, as if I have something for them that they really wouldn't want, and all the time they're screaming at me in Hebrew, screaming different things simultaneously. It's all very confusing, and I have to react swiftly without reacting, if you see what I mean. I don't even notice, or remember, whether their weapons are raised. I only know one word of Hebrew: 'ANGLIT'. English. I say it. One of them gestures at me to move to the side of the road, which I do.

"You are a tourist?" he asks me in English. All Israelis learn it at school as a second language, I am told.
"Yes."
"Open your bag, please."

I acquiesce and pull it open. He sees that there are no wires and batteries and flashing lights down there in the darkness, only a couple of gnarly old travel books.

"Where are you going?"
"To Tel Aviv, to the airport!" I tell him. I'm smiling now, in spite of myself. "I have to go home today. It's Christmas!"
"OK. It's OK," he says turning to his colleague, who is much taller than him and still looks very angry. I'm still not sure whether he is still very suspicious and pissed off at me, or if it's just an amateur good cop-bad cop routine. But they let me through anyway.
"Have a good trip. Merry Christmas!", he calls after me as I walk away. "Cheers!" I say back to him, muffledly and nervous now, half over my shoulder. I keep walking. I'm conscious that I might be shot in the back at any time. Stranger things have happened.

I have to walk for another five minutes or so, down to a major junction and then left to where another taxi will pick me up. Despite numerous requests, they won't come all of the way up to the checkpoint. It's too dangerous. Instead, I have to wait in the freezing cold for a further twenty-five minutes, craning my neck at the taxis and lorries and private cars – which almost all seem to be sporting Israeli flags – hurtling past. One flash motor even slows right down to stare me out as it cruises by, but the moment soon passes.

Eventually a Servis pulls up and I open the front door. The driver gestures for me to put my bags in the back and I comply. There's a book in there but I'm by now too tired and wired on endless instant coffee to concentrate on anything, and I'm also developing quite a hearty bronchial cough.

"Tel Aviv?" I ask him.

"Airport," he replies, and this is his first and final word of English to me. All of the way along the ninety-minute journey the radio drones away to itself in Hebrew, interspersed with occasional references to George Bush, Tony Blair and the Taleban. We stop at about five addresses around the private estates and urban settlements of "greater Jerusalem". At first it occurs to me that I might be about to be either kidnapped or just plain executed. On the top part of the windscreen there is a small photograph of a very traditional-looking orthodox fellow, and I wonder if this mightn't be Rabbi Kahane, the ultra-right Zionist who was gunned down in New York city a couple of years previously. I think of Robert Fisk, always at risk. And then we're back on the Jewish-only freeway.

Appendix 1

As I had been to the West Bank with ISM before my second visit in April 2002, and I had already experienced Tel Aviv's Ben Gurion airport and the hassle that the staff give you there, this time I came through Jordan and across King Hussein Bridge. It's more expensive, with entry and exit taxes that would normally be covered by your flight ticket, but it's worth it if your budget can run to it.

I met other activists in Amman and at the bridge and we took a taxi together, across the edge of the Judean desert and on to Bethlehem. When we reached the main checkpoint we discovered that there had been a curfew in force all day, part of a wider collective punishment for the passover suicide bombing that had taken place in Netanya the night before, and taxi drivers were being angrily turned away by the IDF. A Palestinian friend from the previous campaign happened by, and told us that if we jumped down onto the footpath we could walk around the edge of the checkpoint safely. We took his advice and were almost around the corner and on the home strait when a soldier noticed us and called us back, screaming and levelling his gun at us. We walked back to the road and were standing around on the kerb wondering what we ought to do next when another *servis* - a Palestinian shared taxi – screeched to halt just in front of us.
"OK, get in my friends, it's OK" a *kheffiyed* youth beseeched us, leaning out of the passenger window. "Where do you want to go?"
"We want to go into Bethlehem through here but they're not letting us. There's been a curfew all day. Do you know if any of the other checkpoints are open?" we asked him.

"Yes, Beit Jala checkpoint is open. My sister lives there and I've just spoken to her. Come on, get in! I will take you there."
We agreed a price and piled in, and in less than five minutes we were staring at an obscure little backwater road, completely inaccessible to vehicular traffic. Our guide stepped out of the van and showed us

where to walk, and when we reached the other side another car pulled up and its driver asked us where it was we were off to. He then called us a taxi on his mobile, and soon we were on our way to the Star hotel, close to Manger square. I wondered were we might have been left without this ubiquitous modern miracle, the cellphone. Only a few short years ago, I recalled, many of our demonstrations in England were only just about held together with short-range walkie-talkies.

The next morning was a good enough start. I sat in my shared room in the Star hotel on Star street, the highest point in Bethlehem and one of only two hotels to be built in the West Bank since the occupation began[xlviii], watching television. I was watching the early morning news on CNN, and it was Good Friday. Just before breakfast, Ariel Sharon had called a live council-of-war type press conference with members of his cabinet. He said that Arafat was the enemy, that Israel was "in a war here", and called up 20,000 army reservists in order to 'destroy the terrorist infrastructure'. This would be ostensibly in response to the suicide bombing in Netanya on Wednesday evening, but in actuality a reaction the Saudi peace plan that was formally put forward at the Arab summit on the same day. Sharon is through and through a settlement man, and there's simply no way that he could countenance the IDF leaving the occupied territories while Palestinians are still alive there. He's also a leader who understands only war; elected entirely on a war footing, without it there is simply no reason for his leadership, or even existence.

All Friday morning we were expecting to hear of retaliations in Ramallah, Nablus or even Bethlehem itself. On CNN there were reports of the panic buying of food and water in Ramallah, as the IDF used tank shells to blast two enormous holes through the front wall of president Arafat's governancy building. Later, the Israeli army invaded part of the complex and took it over. There was a firefight with members of Fatah, where the army injured many and eventually 'arrested' some seventy and cut off the phone lines and the electricity. Over the compound's walls heavy earthmoving equipment and tanks could clearly be seen moving around, and there were reports of 'room-to-room fighting' throughout the afternoon. One source also related that seven civilians had been killed by Israeli sniper fire as they ran for their homes when the assault began. Later reports detailed how four P.A. policemen and one IDF soldier were killed in the fighting that followed this, and later – over the ensuing days of the Easter weekend – five Palestinian policemen were executed; taken prisoner alive, and then shot through the head. Then, just after the lunch-break, a further report came in over the telephone of a suicide bombing at a supermarket in west Jerusalem. At first details were unclear, with no reports of any casualties, but later it emerged that two people had been killed in the attack, and that the bomber had been a 16-year old woman from Deheishe refugee camp in Bethlehem. There were also some reports of some fierce fighting close to the Al-Aqsa mosque in Jerusalem's old city, where it was said that ten people had already been killed, including two foreign journalists. This report later turned out to be false, but now it seemed that the tanks would come rolling our way any time soon, and a proposed trip to Ramallah was abandoned as it was now deemed impossible to get into the city, and there were already some internationals present there. Of a lively Italian contingent from Ya Basta!, some thirty were also staying at Deheishe itself. Several options were talked over, but it was finally decided that – as the camp was likely to be due for a major incursion very soon, as is the normal reaction in such cases – a solidarity visit was in order. The weather was torrential and unrelenting, and so a bus was ordered for health reasons. We walked through the camp and saw the terrible conditions, the grey misery, the ruined housing and the absolutely decimated ruins of martyrs' homes. Several banners had been hastily prepared for the occasion, and we chanted as we marched, while some more of the Italians sang anti-state terrorism songs. We marched right up to the top of the hill and we marched back down again, where we came to Al-Ibd'a, the Deheishe social centre. There are 11,000 inhabitants at Deheishe camp, which stands on scarcely one square kilometre of badly paved land. In the area around the camp the roads are patched at intersections with bright yellow sand, filling in the roads for where Israeli shells and bulldozers have torn them up. The centre itself houses a number of projects, mostly for the children of the camp. Jihad, a young Deheishe resident, told us that the centre "lights up all the darks" of life under the occupation. There are two schools in the camp – one for boys and one for girls – and the students are crammed in to study between the breezeblocks, fifty to a class. As you might expect, water is scarce anyway here during the summer months but the IDF often cut it off completely, along with the electricity supply. There are also only one doctor and four nurses for the whole of the camp's residents. The people who live in Deheishe came from some forty-eight villages in the 1948 'war', the *Naqba*, and lived there just in tents until 1952. Some of the refugees came all of the way from Haifa, and after four years under canvas they moved to the corpulent luxury of those three-metre square grey breezeblock shacks, where the whole family would share a single bedroom.

One of the Italians stood up to explain themselves, with the aid of a translator. She said that they were a solidarity group who for the past ten years had been doing work mostly inside Deheishe, helping to build it up and make it work. "Also, this year we came here to stay together with the kids, to help them through and to show our presence here during the occupation. Now we see that the situation is getting worse and worse, and that acts are getting all the more nasty."

Later, the mayor of Bethlehem municipality came to speak with us. He had an assistant to translate for him, and he basically said: "Thank-you for your visit, especially at this moment when Palestinians are suffering the most. Your presence this time reflects how knowledgeable you are about the situation. Welcome to Palestine; a Palestine which is currently being crucified as Jesus once was. You have seen for yourselves that no-one is excluded, from the president to the workers who are excluded from their fields." Just a couple of days later, after the IDF had opened fire on us with live ammunition as we were attempting to march peacefully and silently into the besieged

Bethlehem suburb of Beit Jala – which they had supposedly pulled out of the previous day – he would stop by again at the hotel with his translator, offering us his sympathies for our injuries. Seven of us had been hit by shrapnel, and he furthermore informed us that "your blood was mixed with the blood of the Palestinian people today." Later still, after my return to London, I learned that he had gone into the Church of the Nativity in Manger Square, in order to stand by the local people who had fled there in terror of the IDF, during the invasion that was shortly to come.

on the Friday afternoon, those of us who had been before and knew a little of the workings of the IDF made our way down the hill out of Bethlehem. We marched past Beit Jala hospital towards the little town itself, and when we reached the corner where a small ring-fenced statue of St. George appropriately slaying the dragon welcomes you, we encountered what inadvertently became our quarry - or perhaps us theirs - a couple of APCs. The march came to a halt and all singing and chanting immediately ceased. An APC – Armoured Personnel Carrier – is really no different from a tank, albeit a little smaller. It carries a crew of six soldiers, all armed, dangerous and ready for action, and the only really difference lies in the absence of a gun turret. There seemed to be some confusion at this point as to our precise objective. Were we there to confront the 'tanks', or to march past them into Beit Jala for a solidarity visit? I was of the latter persuasion, but I nonetheless hung around with the others whilst a consensus that never came was reached. The APC's commander seemed to be equally confused. He was waving at us to get back, but employing no verbal directives at all. Everybody seemed to be just milling around. When the bright-orange percussion grenade came, it was hardly a threat: we knew what it was from our training, and had plenty of time to get out of the way and block up our ears. Now our problem was one of inefficient organisation. What did we want to do next? Were we staying with the APCs, were we going to try to march past them to get into Beit Jala proper in solidarity with its poor beleaguered residents, or had we made our point adequately already?

At this point some of our Palestinian organisers were urging us to make a dignified retreat, but the majority of the Italians from Ya basta! seemed intent on staying and possibly staging a sit-down protest in front of the APCs. The point I am making here is not that either position was the incorrect one, but that the objective of our protest should have been decided well in advance of the march, and that it should have been clearly understood by everyone.

The following day passed largely without incident in the Bethlehem locality: but the tension was clearly rising. Although the people were as friendly as ever, armed men from the Tamzim – the local defence militias – were becoming increasingly more visible on street corners. On the Thursday morning, I had woken in my hotel room to a newsflash from CNN. Ariel Sharon and a council of war were holding an aggressive press conference, detailing their intention to now smash the PLO's "terrorist infrastructure" once and for all. Sharon told of how he was calling up 20,000 reservists in this latest brutal operation, purportedly a reaction to the suicide bomb at Netanya, but also curious in its proximity to the Saudi peace plan that had been officially announced at the pan-Arab conference in Lebanon the day before. The television kept alternating between the Israeli cabinet's resolute statements of aggression and the beginning of its reality in Ramallah, where tanks had been shelling the *Mukhata* – President Arafat's famous governancy compound – since 6am. In the days that followed we would learn of the truly horrible actualities of the high council of Zion's mealy-mouthed platitudes. Soon after, five Palestinian Authority policemen would be disarmed and then shot dead in the street in Ramallah in cold blood, and just a couple of days later a similar fate awaited another thirty: lined up, blindfolded and then all machine-gunned to death from a nearby Merkava tank. However, to the best of my knowledge neither of these incidents was ever reported in our mainstream media.

Our Easter was to be spent joining in a march from the Greek Orthodox church – who were commemorating the death of Christ at a slightly later date than their Catholic counterparts – to the Catholic church, in the Bethlehem suburb of Beit Sahour. In spite of a couple of placards depicting Saddam Hussein, and even three or four members of (presumably) Hamas getting on top of a building at the rallying-point of the march, burning a hastily home-made Israeli flag and letting off a few rounds into the bargain, the whole affair passed off without incident. I was able to catch up with a friend from the December campaign, who lives locally and now works as a medic for the Palestinian Red Cross Society. One member of our group wondered aloud to me just what we were doing marching in time to images of the great dictator, but I didn't feel myself fit to judge the political affiliations of those who have to live under the gun.

We had also been spending our nights in the local refugee camps acting as human shields to the impending full-scale invasion. There are three camps in Bethlehem: Al-Azza, Aida and Dheishe. The last two suicide bomb attempts had been conducted by former residents of Dheishe, so this was expected to receive the first of the IDF's attentions when they inevitably came in. However, there was already a presence of some thirty Italians staying there, so we were split between the other two camps. I went to Azza, where our evening's reception and orientation was cut short by bursts of rapid gunfire from the nearby IDF checkpoint. The Israeli army do this day and night, we were told, picking off individuals at random from the camp's main street, but when they started firing into the camp at night it was best to be indoors. Along the walls of the social centre where we were assembled to receive our accommodation details there were posters of their latest victim, a 14-year old Muslim girl. All of the residents of Azza are Muslims, originally Bedouin tribes peoples from the Beer Sheeva region in the upper Negev desert. Myself and my housemate were taken down several dark alleys, running, whispering, and turning back until we finally reached the danger-spot opposite the Paradise hotel at the edge of the camp. Live gunfire rang out sporadically around us. Before we crossed the street, our guide turned to us several times for confirmation. "You understand that they are shooting at us?" he asked. "That you could be killed at any time? You understand this?" We both nodded and then quickly whispered our assent aloud, unused to the darkness. "Then run like a rocket!" we were told.

Once inside with our family, the night passed in relative ease. Occasionally more shots would ring out, but our genial hosts - the brothers Nasser and Yassir - assured us that this was pefectly normal for them, day or night. I managed to capture a little of this on minidisc, but in retrospect it sounds a lot less threatening than Chinese new year, and nothing like the death and grief that it truly portends. My amateur journalist's apparatus was a lot more useful in amusing the children. The next night we were moved into the apartment of a single man, who was due to be married in June 2002, but who hadn't seen his fiancee for over five months as she lives outside of Bethlehem, and he isn't allowed to move freely about in his own country. We were told that we would be safer there, as the apartment was in a central courtyard and shielded by other dwellings. "It will be a tall night!" another young man told us, a Palestinian policeman named Omar who was normally based in Beit Jala but who couldn't be there at that time because it was considered "too dangerous". The IDF had supposedly pulled out of Beit Jala in the days before but, as we had seen, they clearly hadn't. This was taken to be yet another sign of something very major and imminent in the offing. Meanwhile, the media was reporting some 47 IDF tanks being massed at Bethlehem checkpoint for the past two nights. But it wasn't to be a tall night that night. We waited.

Easter Monday was the day before the Israeli army finally came into Bethlehem, but first we were to be treated to a nominal aperitif of their US-sponsored firepower, and their callous disregard for the status of foreign civilians and journalists. We had decided to march back to Beit Jala, and possibly deliver a few supplies to the villagers there. This time the APCs had pulled back along the road into Bethlehem a little, and we were able to walk past the church on the corner of the hill. When we got to about 100 yards from the military presence we again ceased our singing, and two negotiators were nominated to move toward them slowly with hands in the air. These were Lilian Pizzichini, a journalist from east London, and Kunle Ibidun, a peace activist and IT consultant from Bristol. Without warning, live ammunition was fired at the ground just in front of their feet. The bullets fired were later identified as being perforated in order to immediately fragment and cause random injuries without a direct hit being necessary to cause harm: such ammunition is illegal under international law. All of the time that we were pushed down the hill the APC's commander was speaking into a headset, apparently acting on instructions from above. Kunle was hit three times by shrapnel and was taken to the nearby Beit Jala hospital, together with a Palestinian cameraman working for the Al-Jazeera network. More shooting followed with the three APCs moving slowly towards us, moving us down the hill back in the direction of Bethlehem. In the ensuing confusion, a total of seven international civilians were injured, including one who appeared to have been shot directly in the stomach and who had to have the bullet removed in immediate surgery.

Despite this confusion, however, the march moved slowly backwards past the church and at no stage was any panic or anger, apparent. Also covering the demonstration was the BBC's Orla Guerin, who was chased down an alleyway together with her camera crew under rapid fire. Later, following the apparent massacre at Jenin refugee camp, a spokesman for Israel told BBC radio 4's PM programme that the press was being kept out of the area for its own safety. I was amazed that the BBC expressed no reaction at all to this comment. I have to say that I wasn't particularly frightened at the time, but this was only really because I wasn't quite sure what we were being shot at with.

After all of those injured had been released from the hospital, a few of us tried to relax and get a hold of the day's events. Kunle had discovered upon returning to the hotel that his father had just died of a stroke, and was consequently planning to go back to Britain the following day. A friend, who had never wanted to be in direct confrontation with ridiculous levels of military hardware in the first place, would be joining him, but the remainder of us were vowing to stay. I had decided not to go back to Azza camp for a third night in order to catch up on my writing. As the evening wore on people ran round the hotel, busying themselves in readiness of the coming mass incursions. A few could be heard crying or getting a little emotional in other ways behind closed doors, as the reality of what had been done to us during the afternoon sank in. Whilst some dealt with the intense situation by making innumerable lists or locking themselves into broom cupboards, my own contingent dealt with things by drinking all of the beer in the hotel, although to be fair it's a very small bar. The next night, French journalists would take care of the whisky and the brandy. The left-wing comedian, Jeremy Hardy, found that he was able to cope by using his new captive audience to practice his one-liners upon, honing them to perfection. We sat up chatting until about 11:30, when we were informed that the IDF had taken over the Ibda'a social centre at the entrance to Dheishe, and were using the position to shell into the camp. We could now hear Apache helicopter gunships buzzing about over the city intermittently, and we were advised to vacate the restaurant which is on the hotel's 5th floor, is made largely of glass, and is the highest point in Bethlehem. We retired to the lobby downstairs where some Tamzim were just leaving to go out onto the streets. For many of us this was one of the hardest things: knowing that many of these people, with whom we had recently shared jokes and cigarettes, were now going outside to their probable deaths.

We sat up until about three, when it became clear that a shift system was in operation and that it was OK to sleep. I managed to snatch an hour before the invasion started in earnest. For the next couple of nights we would be kept awake by relentless machine-gun fire and the chop-chop-chop of helicopter rotor blades. After the first night the electricity was cut off, and when the hotel manager ventured outside to set in motion his emergency generator, he was shot at by IDF snipers. There was often a tank directly outside of the lobby. We were told to keep the curtains permanently drawn and to stay away from windows, the top floor was now off limits, and a moratorium was put on showers. Once a day we would eat stale pitta bread and local cheese, and occasionally there would be a cooked meal.

Kunle was becoming worried that he would miss his father's funeral, and the British and American consulates were contacted to try to evacuate those who wished to leave. Aisa, a Japanese national, was in constant pain and barely able to walk after being hit three times in the leg by Israeli shrapnel, but was offered only the vague promise of a taxi by her own government. She eventually came out with the Americans. A convoy of armoured vehicles from the two embassies arrived at Bethlehem checkpoint on the second day, but they returned to Jerusalem after three hours of negotiations with the IDF produced no result. By this time, a few more of us were wavering in our resolution to remain come-what-may, as we had by now been in telephone contact with loved ones back home and it was becoming clear that this might be our only opportunity to get out. It was also obvious to me that there was very little that I could do personally, locked down tight in a hotel, unable to move, and consuming other people's food. Late one night a desperate plea had come through from a family in the vicinity of the hotel. They had refused to open their reinforced front door to the IDF, who had fired a volley of armour-piercing bullets straight through it, killing the mother and the eldest son. This had happened two days previously, and the father was left with two mouldering corpses and a brood of hysterical toddlers. There was simply nothing that we could do. As soon as we stepped out of the door we would have become targets for snipers.

The next day the Anglo-American relief convoy, also carrying a little food, arrived again at Bethlehem checkpoint. There were the same protracted negotiations, but this time they were eventually successful. I was first made aware of this by live commentary from CNN, an altogether surreal state of affairs. Don't kill your TV yet. There were now seven 'Brits' wanting to get out, and also a number of Americans. When the convoy eventually arrived, it was even more surreal than the television. Whilst we had only two drivers, the Americans had brought with them a screaming squadron from the US marines. As we drove back towards Israel, past Rachel's tomb, the scale of the IDF's rampage of vandalism became a little more apparent. The streets were flooded, not from any storms but from deliberately smashed water pipes, and they seemed to have driven their tanks over every single street lamp in the city. When the Israelis eventually pulled out of Bethlehem – as I believed at the time that they would surely have to – the cost of rebuilding was going to be immense.

Appendix 2: Dispatches Under Siege.

In the weeks following my return from Palestine in April 2002, I was kept up to date with ongoing events by the Palestinian-American organiser Huwaida Arraf via e-mail, as a member of the Palsolidarity network at Yahoo.com newsgroups. What follows is a contraction of those messages. All dispatches, unless stated otherwise, are from Huwaida herself. Some minor alterations may have been made to the text.

February 7th
Occupation Forces Raid and Attack Nablus Village

Occupation forces raided Osrin Village, 22 km southeast of Nablus, with tanks and armoured vehicles today. Witnesses reported that around 10 armoured vehicles raided the village from all sides under intense fire, and tear gas and sound bombs. Occupation forces also opened fire intensively and randomly at the village's homes. Several people suffered from severe fear and panic. Witnesses reported that children fainted due to the intensity of the tear gas bombs fired. Occupation forces chased Palestinian civilians through the village's side roads and streets.

Colonialist Activities in Jenin

Occupation bulldozers leveled vast areas of agricultural land today along the Jenin-Nablus road and closed all main and side roads leading into Jenin. Witnesses reported that occupation bulldozers supported by tanks carried wide-scale demolitions and closure measures that included closing all main and side roads linking towns and villages Southwest of Jenin.

Land Confiscation and Tree Uprooting in Jerusalem and Bethlehem

Occupation bulldozers opened a new colonialist road (4km long and 10m wide) from Um al-Btein, east of al-Faradis, towards Wa'r Um al-Sousan in al-Ta'amira area. Witnesses reported that Israeli colonists bulldozed three dunums (1dunum=1000m2) and cut over 100 olive trees in Nahalin town, Bethlehem. The land belongs to Palestinian citizen Fahd Najajra.

Witnesses reported that occupation forces and colonists confiscated yesterday around 1000 dunums of land in Janata village, Bethlehem. Colonists under the protection of the occupation army placed 10 caravans in preparation for the constriction of a new colony

Life Threatening and Humiliating Closure Measures

Jenin
Occupation forces closed entrances to the following villages with sand piles, cement blocks and ditches:

- Arraba
- Marka
- Anza
- Al-Zawiya
- Al-Mansoura

In addition, occupation forces prevented anyone from entering the area, considered the only link between over 10 villages. Occupation forces also chased and threatened those attempting to cross on foot.

Nablus
Occupation forces reportedly treated the inhabitants of Beit Forik village in an inhumane manner today. A bus carrying a group of people to Nablus from the town was stopped by occupation forces and the people were forced to stand in two lines. The older people were

forced to run far and back several times and to do gymnastics moves under the threat of weapons. The people also reported that occupation forces asked some of those attempting to cross through the military roadblock established at the entrance of the village (for the past 18 months) to bend over so that the soldiers could kick them. In addition, occupation forces used extremely offensive language toward the inhabitants.

Military reinforcements were reportedly deployed on Mount Jarzeem. Witnesses living nearby reported that occupation forces based on the mount have been bringing in caravans and observation towers. Mount Jarzeem overlooks Nablus city and Balata refugee camp from the south and west and has been used by occupation forces to carry out provocative attacks against Palestinians in the city. Wide-scale bulldozing activities have been carried on the mount, during which dozens of trees and historical remains were demolished.

Qalqilya
Qalqilya and its surrounding villages continue to be isolated from the outside world. Occupation forces based at the many military roadblocks established at the entrances of towns and villages and on main junctions continue to provoke Palestinian civilians and prevent them from crossing. Several people attempting to enter the city through side sand roads on foot were held for several hours by occupation forces under humiliating and threatening measures. Occupation forces attacked civilians in Jit village with dozens of tear gas and sound bombs while they were attempting to head to Nablus and Ramallah through the only exit available.

Ramallah
Occupation forces closed Southwest Ramallah, al-Bireh and the suburbs of Jerusalem, while more military reinforcements were deployed in the al-Irsal area, near President Arafat's headquarters. The newly imposed closure measures isolated over 10 villages. Occupation

Special Forces, disguised as Arabs spread out intensively at the main junctions and entrances.

Witnesses reported that occupation forces practiced humiliating measures against all those attempting to cross from one place to another, regardless of age or sex.

Occupation Makes Life of Palestinian Family a Living Nightmare

The suffering of the Khalil family in Beit Our al-Tahta Village, Ramallah, began last December - during the month of Ramadan - when occupation forces confiscated their five-story house under the threat of weapons and placed 17 members of the family in two unhealthy rooms. They were prevented from moving furniture, food or clothes for their children from their home. Occupation forces also destroyed the family's belongings and threw a major part of them into a nearby well. Ibrahim tried to describe his family's tragic story. "My parents have been forced to watch all that they have worked hard for all their lives be destroyed and are being forced to live in an unhealthy damp closed room."

Ibrahim said that occupation forces purposely destroyed their belongings despite the fact that no one in the family has done anything wrong. He also said that the occupation forces use too much electricity and water on purpose, explaining that their electricity bill came up to 2380 Shekels (around $600) in one month. Ibrahim's brother also said that the family's lives are in danger since occupation forces open fire at any movement to and from the house at night. He said that their house has become an overcrowded cold prison and wondered what gave those soldiers the right to occupy their home and transform it into an observation post with no respect for their lives, their health, or that of their children.
The family called on all international and human rights organisations to help them put an end to the increasing Israeli aggression and to force the Israeli soldiers out of their house after getting them to

compensate for all the damage that they have caused.

Escalation of Provocations at Gaza Military Roadblocks

A Palestinian driver was forced to reverse quickly dozens of meters when an Israeli tank attempted to crash into his car, to distance him from al-Shuhada junction south of Gaza City. The taxi driver helplessly prayed for his life.

Dozens of meters away from the mentioned junction, several tanks and armoured vehicles were placed in the middle of Salah al-Din Street, the main link between north and south, to give way to a bus transporting Israeli colonists and protected by tanks, military jeeps and dogs. The driver, who proved to be a very good one indeed, pointed out that all of these occupation measures are not simply to allow the colonists and their dogs to pass safely as occupation forces claim, but to exert more pressure on the Palestinian people and to show off their overwhelming might in front of women and children.
Following the provocative incident, a state of chaos existed in the place for over half an hour. Occupation forces then forced people to take their clothes off, tore up many of their identity cards and showered them with humiliating language.

Several drivers who transport people between the north and south of the Gaza Strip confirmed that the provocative incident is not the first of its kind. One driver, who preferred to remain anonymous, said that people are forced most of the time to wait for several hours at Israeli military roadblocks for no apparent reason, adding that the line of cars from Khan Younis stretches several kilometres due to the closure of al-Matahin military roadblock south of Deir al-Balah.

The people are often surprised by new occupation military roadblocks called `flying roadblocks". Certain roads are suddenly closed with tanks, and people are forced out of their cars and subjected to humiliating searches before being permitted to cross, in some cases passing in front of life-threatening tanks on foot. Occupation forces continuously place traffic lights and control gadgets on the above-mentioned road, aimed at delaying movement of Palestinians greatly. Several drivers stressed that they have to be alert at occupation military roadblocks and traffic lights set up by occupation forces, to avoid being fired at by soldiers who hide in their tanks and well-shielded cement military points.

Despite all the occupation obstacles, the Palestinian citizens insist on moving between different parts of the Gaza Strip to reach their daily destinations, even if they have to wait for long hours and are subjected to occupation attacks and humiliations. At the same time, occupation soldiers do not dare to get out of their tanks or their highly-secured military locations.

I just got back from Ramallah Hospital, around the corner from my apartment, as two young boys that I had got to know over the course of the three days that the internationals maintained a protest tank in front of Israeli tanks in Ramallah, were shot today by the Israeli occupation forces.

Musa Nuzhi - 12 ½ years old was shot in the head with a rubber-coated steel bullet from a distance of 20 meters. He is currently undergoing minor surgery.

Fadi Kareem – 14 years old was shot in the back with a rubber bullet after soldiers had him surrounded. Three Israeli soldiers grabbed Fadi after they shot him, took him into one of the apartment buildings that they are occupying on Israeli Street and proceeded to taunt and mentally torture him. Soldiers swiped a knife by his legs threateningly, tearing his jeans and slicing his leg. He was also gouged in the face. He was released four hours later and is now recovering. Both of the boys admit to throwing stones at the Israeli tanks and armoured personnel carriers (APCs). This is the soldiers' rationale for opening fire on Palestinian children, aiming for their upper body.

"We just want them out of here" murmured Musa from his hospital bed.

February 22
After the roadblock removal by Palestinians and internationals today, the following took place:

At the entrance to the village, Palestinian youths were throwing small stones towards the main road. One settler driving past got out of his car and pointed his gun at the children, who fled. Soldiers, on duty nearby, assuming the man was a Palestinian, shot him in the head. He subsequently died. Upon learning the identity of the settler, soldiers became enraged and called in backup. Two tanks, 5 jeeps and 23 soldiers on the ground entered Beit Umar firing live ammunition at anything that moved. The tanks and soldiers proceeded to the town centre and continued to shoot live ammunition and tear gas. Three boys were shot in the leg, and one was shot in the shoulder/chest area. All have been hospitalised, with the boy who was shot in the torso undergoing surgery at the moment.

Soldiers noticed in the distance a young child playing with a toy gun given to him as a present for the Eid. They took off after him, and he fled. Arriving at the garden the soldiers confiscated the toy gun, but proceeded to shoot at the door to a nearby house. They tried to enter but couldn't and instead broke the windows to the house and entered that way. The owner of the house was not in the village at the time, so the soldiers rampaged through the house, ransacking it.

The author writes,
While all of this horror was going on, Israeli President Ariel Sharon was facing indictment for – amongst other things – crimes against humanity for his part in the Sabra & Shatila massacres in September 1982 during the Lebanon war, when he was Israeli defence minister. The proceedings were due to take place in an independent court in Belgium, where there is currently a law allowing such proceedings to go ahead in the country, regardless of where the crimes are said to

have taken place. Also at about this time, the principal prosecution witness – former Phalange commander Elie Hobeika – died in mysterious circumstances in Lebanon. That is to say, his car was booby-trapped. What follows is an open letter to the plaintiffs in the case – some of the survivors of the massacre - from US citizen Ellen Siegel, who was working as a nurse in the area at the time.

OPEN LETTER

Printed in As-Safir, March 4, 2002
Ellen Siegel

To my friends in Sabra and Shatila,

I hope some of you remember me.

I came to Beirut in August of 1982 to help. I worked as a nurse at the camp hospital, Gaza Hospital. I took care of many of you. I was there during the massacre.

I remember when I first arrived. You had just made it through three months of horrendous warfare. Conditions in the camp were pretty awful; open sewage system, overcrowding, poverty, and much destruction. There were, as there are now, government rules and regulations in place making it impossible to improve your lives.

It was a privilege for me to know you and learn something about your lives. You are a strong and proud people despite long years of suffering. You remain patient; you endure. You hope that one day the world will realise the validity of your cause and right a wrong. You still believe that one day you will be able to use that door key you have kept from your home in Palestine.

I had never practised my profession in such horrendous conditions. I had never worked in a hospital that lacked water much of the time, that had an electrical system that operated only periodically, that had windows partially or completely blown out by explosions, and that was devoid of even the simplest of medical supplies and clean linen. But I must tell you: it was the most fulfilling and satisfying experience of my nursing career. After work I used to stroll down the main thoroughfare of the camp, Sabra Street. I would buy cigarettes, juice, bottled water, and trinkets from the vendors. I visited many of your bombed-out homes, enjoyed a cup of Arabic coffee with you. You always made me a welcome guest.

To end Israel's assault on you, my government brokered an agreement between Israel and the PLO. Israel would cease its war on you if you would agree to the departure of many of your husbands, brothers, fathers and sons. These men would be exiled from your homes and neighbourhoods to some far-off Arab country. You were told you would be safe without them. We all know what happened then. The Phalange militia, your avowed enemy, knowing you were unprotected, came to visit and wreck havoc upon you. They stayed for at least 48 hours, maybe more. All the while, the Israel Defence Force (IDF) under the command of Ariel Sharon, surrounded the camps. They provided the flares that we all saw going off - the ones that lit the sky so that the militia could find you. And the bulldozer that many of us saw covering up the bodies of your loved ones where the mass grave is – that, too was supplied by Israel. It seems the IDF was aware early on of at least some of what was happening in the camps and did nothing to stop it. I do not need to remind you of the details. Suffice it to say that when the raping and brutal killings ended, you lost over a thousand - maybe many more – of your loved ones.

When it was over, journalists and photographers descended on the camp. You became the news of the day.

The Israeli government established a Commission of Inquiry. You eagerly awaited the commission's findings. After all, the largest demonstration in Israel's history had taken place shortly after the massacre. A majority of Israelis were calling for an official investigation into how this could have happened, how the Jewish state could be involved in such a thing. The result was that Sharon was found to bear personal but indirect responsibility. He was mildly reprimanded. He did not serve any time in prison for this crime. So no justice was served here.

Lebanon, because of its complicated political situation, has been unable to try those deemed responsible. So no justice served there.

For a time you had hope that at last the Palestinians' problem would be resolved in a just manner. After all, there was Madrid, the Oslo Accords, and Arafat at the White House; then there were more negotiations and agreements.

In February 2001, Ariel Sharon was elected Prime Minister of Israel. The relationship between Israel and the Palestinians has deteriorated rapidly ever since. Sharon continues to surround your people and perpetrate acts of violence against them.

Whenever I see or hear from someone who has been to the camps, I ask after you. I hear that conditions are even worse than when I was there. I am told how terrible and miserable life is for you. Always, the person I ask has tears in their eyes.

Even the mass gravesite, which in my country would be hallowed ground, turns into a garbage dump from time to time. It seemed as if the world forgot you. Then, in June of 2001, the BBC aired a film about the massacre. Around the same time, some of you filed a formal complaint in Brussels charging Sharon and others with war crimes, crimes against humanity, and genocide. There is a renewed interest in you and in taking a closer look at what happened in September 1982.

It has been almost 20 years since those terrible days. I, too, have lived with the memories of this atrocity all these years. Unlike you, I was able to leave the camp and return to my home in the United States. I have not had to live as an unwelcome guest in a land that I was not born in. Most importantly, I am not waiting to return to my home.

We are on the eve of a decision by the Belgium Court of Appeals. On March 6 this court is scheduled to announce its decision regarding the legality of the proceedings against Sharon. On February 14 the International Court of Justice issued a ruling. It ruled that all Ministers are immune for all crimes while they are still in office. This means that there is a possibility that the case against Sharon will be dropped. Even the judges of the World Court have failed you. For those of you who survived, for those who lost loved ones, I know you are waiting for justice to be served.

My friends, as we continue to wait, let us remember and honour the victims.

My thoughts are with you,
Ellen Siegel
Washington, DC
February, 2002

March 8th:
Four-year-old Ahmed Khader's heart raced with fear; the children of the neighbourhood told him that we were the Israelis back in his home. The eight of us were not occupation soldiers. Rather we were foreign civilians (5 Americans, 2 Belgian and one Irish) who had come to the Balata Refugee Camp to express our solidarity with the people who had been invaded, terrorised and pillaged on a 4-day raid of their home – a refugee camp – by the Israeli military.
The Israeli Armed Forces had just pulled out of the camp that very morning of Monday March 4, 2002 when we arrived, and Ahmed, who had been locked in one room (8' X 10') with other members of his family for the 4 days of the Israeli raid, feared that they had returned.

Ahmed's aunt explained that we were friends, and the boy cautiously warmed to us. Ahmed wouldn't talk about what had happened to them. He did however admit that he was scared, that he "wasn't brave." Four days earlier, armed Israeli soldiers had broken into the Khader home and ordered the 3 women (including one pregnant and one elderly) and the three children aged 4-9 years that were in the home, into one room. They then proceeded to take over the rest of the home. For the next 24 hours the women and children sat in the room, without food, without relief. And since the Israeli army had cut the electricity in the entire camp, little Ahmed and his family sat in the dark. The soldiers did once give the family the option to leave, but promised them that they would never come back. Already refugees and with nowhere else to go, the family stayed. The next day the soldiers gave permission to the women and children to go to the bathroom and for one of the women to quickly make sandwiches for the kids....

We walked into a small, meagre home, where an elderly woman was sitting on the floor – a static-filled television set the only piece of furniture in the small room. The woman turned to us crying as news of Bushra Abu Kweik and her children's killing* was being reported on the television screen. "They're killing all of our beautiful children. They already took our homes and now they come after us in our refugee camps..." I asked her if the Israeli soldiers had come into her home and she pointed to the gaping hole in the wall behind me... **

Everyone in the streets wanted us to see the damage that had been done to their homes and shops. It was not possible to see it all. Balata is home to approximately 22,000 Palestinian refugees who had been forced out of their homes in 1948, from towns and villages in what is now called Israel. All had been abused and traumatised again by the Israeli Armed Forces. Everyone had a story. All of the homes we saw were severely damaged - windows blown out, walls dynamited as soldiers moved from home to home, with some homes completely destroyed....

In the narrow streets and alleyways of the camp, people could be seen clearing away rubble. An elderly dark-skinned man began talking to me. "I lost my son, my mother and my home, but I still thank God. I have my humanity." Although I was running late for an appointment I stepped into what remained of this man's home where I was introduced to his 12 daughters. A week earlier, Abdallah's son was killed by Israeli forces surrounding Nablus. Abdallah's mother died two days later. The next day, the Israeli Army entered his home. "I tried to speak to the soldiers in Hebrew as I've worked in Israel for over 30 years and know Israelis and Hebrew well. One soldier saw a poster of my slain son on the wall and put out his cigarette butt in between my son's eyes in the photo. He called him a terrorist and said he deserved to die as we all [Palestinians] do." Abdallah's daughters quickly forgot their reserve and began hurling questions, statements and accusations at me: "The American president says we're the terrorists, but who's doing the terrorising?" What kind of people would steal the gold off a woman who has so little? On top of taking our homes, killing our sons and coming after us in our refugee camps, they take women's gold! You tell them. You tell the world that we're not the terrorists. We want our freedom and we will not give up our land. Never." "I'm glad my mother died when she did," said Abdallah. *An Israeli tank shell fired from the settlement of Psagot targeted the car of Bushra and her children in the Amaari refugee camp. The Army was out to assassinate Bushra's husband, Hussein Abu Kweik. **Israeli soldiers used cutting machines to meticulously rip through the walls of the homes and move from home to home. In the refugee camp only a single wall separates most homes.

Adam Shapiro
The first thing you notice at the entrance to the Balata Refugee Camp is the overturned, burned out car stuck in a huge man-made crater in the ground. But this was the battleground of the previous three days, as the Israeli Army sacked the camp and destroyed homes, cars, property, and lives with wanton abandon and without much purpose.

Other than to attack and terrorise a people who have nothing in this world and who have already been made homeless – and who have remained refugees for over 50 years.

Inside the camp, this alleged "hotbed of terrorism" the group of us eight internationals were met and greeted by the residents with inquisitive looks, "salaam aleikum" shouted from time to time, and lots of little kids running up to us to see who were these strangers. All tried to make us feel welcome and when they learned that we were there in solidarity with the people of the camp and wanted to take pictures to show the world, we were pulled in many different directions at once to witness what the Israelis had done.

What they had done was obvious, and it was all over the camp. Immediately noticeable, at eye level, was the black spray paint on the walls – arrows, numbers, Hebrew writing and stars of David, markings the soldiers made to allow themselves to navigate through the crowded camp. Permanent markings of the three days of hell the camp endured. We later found these markings inside people's homes as well, painted on the walls.

Thirty homes were destroyed in the camp, but hundreds more effectively ruined and damaged. The camp is densely populated and some alleyways between the buildings are barely wide enough for me – an average sized male – to pass through. Other structures are just built wall-to-wall. When the Israeli army took down a building – allegedly looking for weapons or rockets (no evidence of any was found) – it meant that the neighbours' buildings were also damaged. The first place I visited was a destroyed home. Next door, the building was still standing, but upon walking in I discovered that the neighbour had lost his wall. The home was also damaged by the demolition and the home made utterly unusable. If each house demolished results in the two or three neighbouring buildings also being damaged beyond use, then the result is between 90 and 120 structures affected. Each structure contains at least two (and usually more) apartments, housing anywhere from 10 to 40 people. Therefore, at minimum, 900 people were left homeless by the demolitions in the camp – this is the calculus of Israel's war on the Palestinian people.

Walking through the streets of the camp, destruction was all around us. Peering down alleyways, we inevitably spotted the chunks of stone, the twisted metal and the broken pieces of furniture that indicated a home was demolished. Cars had been set ablaze and riddled with bullet-holes – the carcasses lay in the streets as added testimony to the siege. Every house we visited had a story to tell. Some were simply shot up, others had tear gas thrown inside, while others were invaded and occupied by the soldiers.

We visited one home that had been occupied during the entire siege by Israeli soldiers. Upon entering the house, the soldiers offered to allow the family to leave, but promised them they would never come back to the house. The family stayed – three children (aged 4 to 9), two young women (one pregnant) and an elderly woman. The man of the house – PLC member and leading figure in the camp, Hussam Khader – was not home for fear of his life. The soldiers forced the family into one room – approximately 8x10 feet – and made them stay there the entire three days. For the first twenty-four hours, not a single person was allowed to leave the room at all – not for the bathroom, not for food, not for water. The soldiers ransacked the entire place – taking money and computer disks, breaking furniture and emptying drawers, ripping apart passports and overturning children's beds. We knocked at the door of the home when we arrived. As we entered the sitting room, we heard a child whimper – little Ahmed (four years old) was afraid we were the Israelis coming back to the house. He is traumatised by the experience and needs to be near his mom and aunt constantly. But he is tough, and before long he was playing with my camera. He told me to follow him upstairs and there he showed me how the soldiers had ransacked his room. He was amazed by the sight and asked me why the soldiers did this to him.

The last home we visited in the camp was located on the main street, near the cemetery. A ground floor apartment was located adjacent to a store. The main gate of the store was blown apart and the glass from the window lay in the street. The back wall of the small store was torn down and you could see directly into the apartment behind – but there was not much to see. Walking into the house we were unable to step on the floor directly – it was covered with clothing, broken dishes, broken furniture, and more. The electricity was cut, so we had to poke around in the diminishing light until a portable fixture was brought in. The lit room revealed the full destruction – even the washing machine was not safe from the brutality of the soldiers. A fully veiled young woman (only her eyes showed) boldly came up to me and asked if I spoke English. I replied that I did and that she could speak to me in either English or Arabic. She explained that she was the oldest of four children in the house – 14-years old – and that her father was dead. She led me over to where the kitchen had been and searched in the broken glass for something. Finally, she pulled up a picture frame with a photo of her father in it and explained to me that Israeli spies had killed him in 1994. In a flash she was back in the pile on the ground looking for another photo – that of her grandfather, also dead. Now holding both pictures, this young Muslim woman, proud to know English and proud of her family, calmly explained what had happened when the soldiers came – how they had to flee and spend the night outside the camp in the nearby fields. For more than fifty years they had been refugees, and now Israel wanted to attack them again. But, she told me, struggling with her emotions and her sense of dignity, "they must know we are strong children and we won't leave this land, my grandfather's land. We will return to the land which they occupied in 1948."

These refugees, like those in the other camps, have lost everything and live with virtually nothing. Now, day after day, the Israeli army is going after them in a pogrom deliberately designed to provoke and to strike terror into the hearts of an entire people. Like little Ahmed Khader, the world must ask, why are the Israelis doing this?

March 12th:

Ramallah saw an invasion of around 150 Israeli tanks and armoured vehicles and thousands of troops at around midnight last night. Israel's targeting of journalists is becoming more overt, in parallel to its attacks on refugee camps. This morning at 8:02AM ET, on CNN's American Morning, veteran correspondent Ben Wedeman reported two incidents to host Paula Zahn where Israel appeared to be targeting journalists and their cameras in Ramallah:

"Paula, that is the City Inn Palace, which is really right across the street from the refugee camp I mentioned. According to our cameraman there, Joe Duran (ph), there were about 40 journalists in the hotel, and they were concentrated in the stairwell on the fourth floor overlooking the camp. Their cameras were rolling. They were all there, and all of a sudden, there were shots coming in their direction from street level from an armoured personnel carrier. They dove out of the way, but exactly the spot where all of the cameras were, was hit by that gunfire.

One ABC camera took seven bullets, including one bullet directly in the lens. The Israeli government subsequently apologised. They said it was a mistake. That they were shooting in an area they believed fire was coming from. But the journalists who were there told me that there was no fire coming from that hotel.

Now, also in another incident, and in fact, the building I am in, Israeli helicopters apparently fired upon it. This camera took five bullets, essentially destroyed. This is where the bullets came out of. No explanation from the Israeli army as to why that incident took place. But I can tell you that this area, Ramallah, has been declared a closed military area by the Israeli defence forces. But we are unable to leave the area, because it is simply too dangerous.

There is a lot of firing going on right now. It's quiet, but over the last hour or two, Paula, there has been some very heavy exchange of fire and also tank fire as well..."

Military tactics used more intensively, include:

* Use of heavy weaponry in intensive strikes, including ground missiles and tank shells from tanks, missiles from helicopter gunships and F-16 warplanes, deployment of tanks, armoured personnel carriers, and heavily armed paratroopers, and use of high velocity live ammunition;

* High numbers of civilian casualties and fatalities, as a result of the disproportionate and lethal use of force in contravention of the Fourth Geneva Convention. Between 28 February 2002 to 10 March 2002 at least 113 killed and 368 injured. Since September 2000 to date 1,160 Palestinians killed and 18,307 injured.

* Assassinations carried out during these operations where arrests or other means of restraint could have been used. Since November 2000 to 11 March 2002 at least 70 have been assassinated, along with at least 20 bystanders (including 5 children).

* Mass arbitrary arrests of all male Palestinians between age about 14 to about 48 years. The detainees, including children, have apparently been arbitrarily arrested, and held in detention camps outside their areas before it is determined whether they should be held or even questioned for suspected 'terrorist' activity, contravening their rights against arbitrary arrest and detention. Since 28 February 2002 to date about 2,200 have apparently been arbitrarily arrested and detained. Cruel, inhuman and degrading methods used during these mass arrests have included blindfolding, hand-cuffing, strip-searching with removal of upper clothing, and writing of numbers on their arms (*reported by the BBC and Ha'aretz, 12 March 2002*).

* Extensive destruction of property, wantonly and without military

necessity, with destruction and/or damaging of civilian homes, workplaces, hospitals, ambulances, field clinics, schools, universities, churches and mosques; key infrastructure including water pipes/supplies and electricity lines. New methods used since Balata have included the destruction of all the walls between adjoining homes as soldiers move from house to house. Family homes have been blown up or otherwise destroyed by Israeli forces in situations where they state that "suspects" have been in those homes, rather than attempting to enter and arrest the purported suspects.

* Access to vital services and supplies, such as electricity, water and food have been restricted or denied altogether, exacerbating the existing humanitarian crisis in all areas.

* Movement of Palestinian vehicles throughout the West Bank has been banned since about 8 March 2002, except for those with express permission. Those travelling without such permission are being shot on sight without warning. Ambulances are also being attacked and denied permission to reach injured and sick patients or move them to hospitals. This ban intensifies the pre-existing severe restrictions on movement (including the hundreds of checkpoints; unmanned dirt blockades and trenches, and few iron gates) and siege that have made access to work, schools, universities, food and water, and other key humanitarian and health services severely restricted if not impossible, since September 2000.

* Attacks on paramedics, medical staff and patients in ambulances, field clinics and hospitals have intensified. Since 28 February 2002 to date it is estimated that about 6 paramedics have been killed, 12 injured and 5 ambulances totally destroyed, and 10 partially damaged. From September 2000 to 1 March 2002 the PRCS estimate that about 165 of their ambulances have been attacked with about 69 destroyed (c. 68% of their fleet); about 122 emergency medical personnel injured. It is estimated that from September 2000 to 6 March 2002, about 17 medical staff have been killed. The

hindering and denial of access to humanitarian assistance and medical treatment are in violation of international humanitarian law. Deliberate attacks constituting wilful killings or wilfully caused serious injuries committed against the wounded or sick, or "against those medical or religious personnel, medical units or medical transports which are under the control of the adverse Party", constitute grave breaches (i.e. war crimes) of article 147 of the Fourth Geneva Convention and article 85, Protocol 1 to the Geneva Conventions. The International Committee of the Red Cross and PRCS have publicly stated that all ambulances were clearly marked and were co-ordinating their movements closely with the Israeli authorities. Physicians for Human Rights-Israel lodged a second petition in the Israeli High Court on 9 March 2002 on the issue of Israeli attacks on ambulances and prevention of evacuation. LAW, MIFTAH and PCHR have condemned the so-called "justification" of all these methods that violate international humanitarian law, being used on the flimsy pretext of rooting out "terrorists" and "terrorist bases". The attacks are being used in effect to punish the entire, defenceless population. Moreover, so-called security or military purposes cannot justify these methods employed that constitute violations of international humanitarian law, in particular where they constitute grave breaches of the Fourth Geneva Convention and Protocol 1 to the Conventions (i.e. war crimes).

The organisations referred to key violations of international humanitarian law and apparent grave breaches (war crimes) they are documenting during the course of these operations, including wilful killings, wilfully depriving protected persons of rights of fair and regular trial, disproportionate use of force intended to cause "great suffering or serious injury to body or health", as well as "extensive destruction and appropriation of property, not justified by military necessity and carried out unlawfully and wantonly." The organisations also referred to other forms of grave breaches (war crimes) that are being perpetrated as a result of the massive attacks against the

Palestinian civilian population, and through the denial or restrictions in access to key food, water supplies and humanitarian aid, including "making of the civilian population the object of attack", launching of "indiscriminate attacks affecting the civilian population or civilian objects in the knowledge that such attacks will cause excessive loss of life, injury to civilians or damage to civilian objects", "making non-defended localities and demilitarised zones the object of attack", making persons the "object of attack in the knowledge that [they are] hors de combat", and "making the clearly-recognised historic monuments, works of art or places of worship which constitute the cultural or spiritual heritage of peoples and to which special protection has been given, the object of attack".

LAW, MIFTAH and PCHR have urged the international community to immediately intervene by:

* Undertaking to unequivocally denounce these brutal actions, in particular the grave breaches of the Fourth Geneva Convention (i.e. war crimes);

* Ensuring the Israeli occupying power's respect of its obligations by taking effective measures, in particular economic sanctions such as the immediate suspension of key trade agreements including the EU-Israel Association Agreement;

* Ending these grave breaches of the Fourth Geneva Convention (war crimes) and other serious violations of international humanitarian law by immediately sending an independent, effective international protection presence to the area;

* Providing an alternative that is capable of dealing with the core of the problem and ending the Israeli occupation, illegal settlement policies and providing refugee rights of return.

* Complying with their own obligations by:

i) investigating, and bringing the perpetrators of such war crimes to trial, and by establishing a War Crimes Tribunal to prosecute such war criminals;
and

ii) ending all aid used to perpetrate such crimes in particular by ending the supply of all arms used against the Palestinian civilian population.

March 17th:

I have not been able to write to you all for a few days. I was without electricity for the three days that Ramallah was invaded and reoccupied by the Israeli military.

When I first heard the gunshots and the advancing tanks at approximately 1:00am on the morning of Tuesday, March 12, I quickly ran to my computer to write. Before I had a chance to finish typing "RAMALLAH UNDER INVASION", the power was cut. Everything went dark and heavy shooting outside my apartment ensued. Why would the Israelis bring their tanks here? I live in a completely civilian area, directly behind the main hospital in Ramallah; a quiet neighbourhood. In fact, the owner of the building promised us quiet when we were looking at the place 5 months ago. But there they were - Israeli tanks and Armoured Personnel Carriers (APCs) rolling down our streets. Bang! Bang! - the sound of Palestinian gun-wielding young men trying to ward off the advancing Israeli army with Kalishnikov rifles and shot guns. Boom! Boom! Boom! Boom! Boom! - Israelis fired their machine guns and BOMB! - a tank shell. Adam (my fiancée) and I hit the ground and from then on, manoeuvred around the house on our hands and knees, not wishing to catch any bullets that might come flying through our window. What to do? I called CNN. Did they know? "Hello, CNN? Do you know the Israelis are invading Ramallah? The tanks are on my street and heading towards the centre of the city." "Are you sure they're headed for the centre of the city and are not just going after the

Amaari refugee camp[1] ." "Yes! I'm sure. They're rolling towards the centre of the city. I see them!"

And for the rest of the night, the sound of heavy bombardment: helicopters flying overhead, tanks rolling in, tank shells being fired, machine guns...And in response, Palestinian shotguns. Explosions. Where? How far? Oh gosh! What was blown up? The Israelis have already caused so much damage, so much destruction. I called my family in the US to reassure them. "Hi Mary, what's up? Listen, when you watch the news and hear that Ramallah has been invaded, don't worry. I'm just fine." "Heidi (my nickname), why don't you just come home?" asked my younger sister. She later told my mother, who then called me pleading with me to come home. She heard the gunfire in the background. She hyperventilated.

I managed to fall asleep for a couple of hours. When I next looked out the front window, there was an Israeli tank pointing its barrel right at my building. An Armoured Personnel Carrier was driving around and a soldier spoke over a loud speaker: "This area is under curfew. All men between the ages of 16-45 years, come out of your homes with your hands up. People in the hospital (which is right behind my house), listen up. All men between the ages of 16-45 years are to come out with their hands up now. You have 5 minutes." Nothing. No one came out. I waited. Then what? Would they try to enter the hospital? They might have tried to advance on the hospital for heavy firing then came from behind our building - Bang! - Bang! Boom! - Boom! - Boom! - Boom! - BOMB! BOMB! for the rest of the day.

In the nearby refugee camp of Amaari, I have some friends. I called to check on the situation there. Were they surrounded like we were? Yes, the Israelis had invaded. They had blown up 3 homes and were rounding up the young men in the camp. Why does Ariel Sharon have a free hand to do this? He has already invaded and terrorised a half-dozen Palestinian refugee camps, in the past few days alone has killed over a hundred men, women, and children, has taken away over 1,300 Palestinian young men, and was now coming into Ramallah to continue his reign of terror. Of course he could! He has a large and powerful army and the Palestinian don't. The international community has yet to show any good-faith efforts to uphold its obligations under international conventions and laws. Leaders were paying lip service to the Palestinian people, but no one was doing anything, and no one was going to do anything; so Ariel Sharon was going to invade, destroy and kill with impunity and with no boundaries.

March 13

With still no electricity, rumours that our water supply was going to be cut because the Israeli army had destroyed a main water pipe, and fighting still going on outside, I decided to try and leave my apartment to meet a journalist who was making her way into Ramallah. "I'll see you in 10 minutes, insha'Allah (God willing) if I make it." My fiancée and I walked past a number of tanks and smashed cars, crumbled walls and bullet-riddled buildings to make our way out to the main road. We met the journalist at a point where she couldn't take her car in any further - the main road leading into the centre of Ramallah was upturned. A large trench was dug across the road, a water pipe had been cut and water was gushing all over the rubble of the road. As I greeted my guest journalist, other journalist acquaintances warned me to be careful as Israeli snipers were stationed in many buildings and would have no problem shooting at us. "The army opened fire on a group of journalists yesterday and today killed an Italian journalist." "I'll be careful," I said, as if I had any control over whether or not an Israeli soldier would decide to shoot me.

I showed the journalist around the almost deserted streets of Ramallah. Children would peek out of the windows of their homes and wave. A look of disbelief showed on the faces of the adults who must have thought us crazy. We walked by a home and noticed an elderly woman standing in the doorway. "Do you know where I can get bread?" she asked. "Not really ma'am. I haven't seen an open shop or bakery." Across the street a man hollered to get my attention. "Can you help us get food?" he asked from the window of him home. We have 80 people living in this building and we are out of food." "Sir, did you call the Red Crescent? Perhaps they are organising food convoys," I responded. How would I be able to get food to the thousands of people that surely needed it by myself? I didn't even see one open bakery. However, I also knew that the Red Crescent was having trouble getting their ambulances to the injured due to Israeli blockades and fire. They surely would not be organising food convoys. Perhaps the Red Cross? I called the Red Crescent to check and sure enough they confirmed that they were having trouble manoeuvring their ambulances and they were waiting for the Red Cross to somehow co-ordinate something with the Israeli military.

Gunfire could be heard from many different directions and we were standing in the middle of the deserted city centre. The Palestinian security, turned resistance fighters, were the only other people in the streets. My journalist friend wanted to interview one of these young men. "Aren't you afraid to die" she asked him. "No. Life under occupation and death is the same thing. I must fight for my freedom and for the liberation of my country. If I can't live free, there's no reason to live. I'm not living right now."

We made our way over to the Qadoura refugee camp. Evidence of the Israeli tanks having made their way through the narrow streets of the camp was prevalent. Electricity poles were knocked over, as were the walls of the home of our next interviewee. I began talking to little Wael. Two years old, he wasn't really talking, just looking at me and laughing bashfully. "He wouldn't stop screaming and crying yesterday" his father told me. "Today it's a little easier." I heard the young woman being interviewed by the journalist start to sob. "The worst thing is the feeling of helplessness. Your kids look to you to protect them and you can't."

Our last stop was the Amaari refugee camp. Although the journalist was getting a little nervous and anxious to get back to Jerusalem, we made our way into the camp en route. Tens of young children ran up to us as soon as they saw us entering. The kids knew Adam and I from previous visits to the camp and from various protest actions we had organised, including soccer games in front of occupying Israeli forces. An older woman grabbed my arm. "Are you going to help us? Can you find out where our men are? They took my son and my husband and I'm left here with the little children, waiting. I don't know....I don't know...." The heavy sound of tanks rumbling could be heard on the next street over. Another woman peering down at me from her home asked, "Can you just check up on our young men? Can you find out what they did to them?" "They took them yesterday," a 12-year-old boy by the name of Mahmoud told me. "They took my father and my uncle," he whispered. The journalist stopped to talk to a boy who was subjected to the round up but had been released. He was 15 years old.

"The Israeli soldiers came around demanding that all men between the ages of 16 and 45, report to the boys school.[2] I'm only 15, but I have an ID card, so I didn't want to take a chance. The soldiers announced that they would be conducting house searches and if they found anyone within age that hadn't voluntarily turned himself in, he would face harsh punishment, and maybe even death. So I went to the school. The soldiers were taking us in one by one. They forced us to strip down to our underwear for searches. Then we were led into this room where we were asked questions about who the activists in the camp were and who in the camp had weapons. Then we were gathered in the schoolyard and made to remain there, with our hands tied above our heads. I was there from 11am until about 7pm. I started to cry and felt like I was going to pass out. I was cold and hungry. I had pleaded with the soldiers earlier, telling them that I was just a child and couldn't take this, but they didn't listen. When I finally broke down crying and looked like I was going to faint, one soldier told me that I could go home. Just me. The rest stayed and I don't know what happened to them. There were about 300 of us."

What could I do for the woman who asked me to check on the men? What could I do for Mahmoud whose father was taken? What could I do for the thousands that were husbandless, childless, fatherless? I knew where they were. The Israeli army was taking these men to their bases. In all likelihood they were being physically abused, if not tortured.

The children wanted to continue walking with us, but as we approached the edge of the camp, the Israeli tank blocking the entrance could be seen. "You guys please stay behind. I don't want these soldiers shooting at you so don't get near them. If I hear that one of you gets hurt, I'll come back here and kill you myself," I said trying to smile. "It'll be OK. It'll all be OK."

[1] The previous weeks had seen the Israeli Armed Forces surround and invade Palestinian refugee camps in Nablus, Jenin, Tulkarem, Gaza and Bethlehem, arresting hundreds of young men and causing large-scale destruction, injury and death. The Israelis claimed that these invasions of refugee camps were "operations" designed to capture Palestinian militants.

[2] The Israeli soldiers occupied the schools in the camp and used them for their base. In Ramallah City, one of the main boy's schools was used by the army as a command post.

Adam Shapiro

The other day, I was riding back to Ramallah from Jerusalem, when the van I was in stopped at the Al-Ram checkpoint - still a couple of miles from the next checkpoint at Qalandiya which serves as the "gateway" to Ramallah. All the traffic was stopped. The Israeli policemen that maintain the checkpoint had shot dead a 11-year old boy who was laying face down on the street, blood flowing onto the pavement. They claimed he was carrying a bomb in his backpack. So no one was allowed to get near, not an ambulance, not the boy's mother. Of course, he was not carrying any such thing - he was on his way home from school, another innocent victim of Israel's racist policies that maintain that all Palestinians are terrorists.

After an hour, I walked around the entire area, and then entered another van to go the rest of they way to Qalandiya. Everyone was talking about what had happened. But they were troubled to find the right word to put on it - criminal, terrible, horrible, an atrocity. It struck me then, that these words are insufficient to describe what had just happened and what was happening throughout the Palestinian territories. And then I thought it is not just these types of words were insufficient, other words had no meaning anymore, such as "terrorist" or "response" or "incitement" or "cease-fire." It seems that our very vocabulary is a victim of Israel's aggression against the Palestinian people.

In sitting down to compose this essay, I quickly scanned my email for any new messages. There was one from my friend Lina from Tulkarem, whose uncle was killed in the recent Israeli invasion of her city. He bled to death in the street after soldiers shot him and refused to allow medical personnel to attend to the injured in the streets. Naturally, Lina is having a hard time dealing with this tragedy (another word that has been robbed of its meaning). So I opened the letter and read the forwarded message from Lina's aunt. It read, I would like to share the story told to me by Em' Naif, your Grandmother, Ziad's mother, when she lost her 1st son Mamoun, 15yrs of age, in the Intifada-the "Resistance", on Easter Sunday, many years ago...Mamoun snuck out of the house to hang the Palestinian flag from a telephone pole in the middle of the night, he was shot dead. Mamoun, @ 15 became the 1st "martyr" of Tulkarim... His body was found the following morning. The men of the family in the "Jarrad quarter"- carried the body home. Em Naif prepared Mamoun to be buried & when the men were carrying his body to the grave they were all arrested & taken to the school & kept prisoners...The soldiers imposed curfew on the "Jarrad quarter"... After a few weeks, when the curfew was lifted, Em Naif left her home to go downtown Tulkarim to check on her older sister- a widow who had been ill...At the time, the streets of the city were blocked off by barrels full of cement...soldiers standing guard on rooftops...As she walked the streets to her sister's home, a soldier jumping from rooftop to rooftop- Fell...He lay in a broken pile at her feet- he softly whispered "mama, mama..." Em Naif took my hands in hers & told me "there is NO difference between this boy & my son Mamoun."

After reading this story, told to Lina to encourage her not to give in to hatred and anger, I realised that there is still one word that has maintained its meaning - mainly because it is not used too often here. That word is "human." While the events of this story transpired during the 1987-1993 Intifada, I know that events like this still take place today - like the number of settlers (yes, even settlers) attended to by Palestinian medics from the Palestinian Red Crescent Society, even as they are being shot at by the Israeli army. Or the offer some months ago when a banquet hall building collapsed and the Palestinian Authority offered its ambulances to assist with the rescue operation (refused by Israel).

Occupation is based on dehumanisation. That is how soldiers are able to do what they do - they are taught and encouraged not to see the Palestinians as humans. I do not believe that Israeli soldiers are inherently evil, but I do believe that when they are serving in the Occupied Territories, or flying their planes and helicopters and bombing cities, they leave their own humanity behind, and therefore are unwilling and unable to see the humanity in the people they are oppressing. For if they did, it would all come crumbling down - like the soldier two weeks ago who left his post, refusing to continue carrying out dehumanising orders.

When Israel finally understands that the occupation is the root cause of the conflict here, and acts accordingly to remove it and allow the Palestinians to live in freedom, the words we need to use to explain and understand our world will once again have meaning. Until then, "human" will remain a word with meaning but without application, and the suffering of a people will continue.

March 19th:
By Aviv Lavie

If and when Anthony Zinni ever finishes his shuttles between Ariel Sharon and Yasser Arafat, a reporter dealing in security affairs joked yesterday, he might want to try solving the problems between the IDF Spokesman's Office and the TV channels, particularly Channel Two. It looks like the two sides need a creative mediator. The latest storm was caused by a report broadcast on Friday night and then rerun on Saturday night, on Channel Two's news show. It showed an IDF force taking over a house in the Al-Ayida refugee camp. During the briefing before entering the house, the soldiers are told to break down the door with a hammer, and if that didn't work, to use an explosive brick. That's what they do. The result: The mother of the family is mortally wounded and lies on the floor, bleeding. The children stand behind her, choking back tears. The father tries calling an ambulance, but it is trapped between checkpoints. The soldiers continue moving through the house, and break into the next house by cutting through the wall. The daughter begs them not to break the wall, but they ignore her. One of the family members asks the soldiers a question, and is shouted at to shut up. To top it all off, one of the soldiers says to the cameras, "I don't know what we're doing here. Purification. Apparently it's dirty here. It's not clear to me what a Hebrew soldier is doing so far from home." The report's power lay in the matter-of-fact manner in which the incident was documented. The soldiers did not depart from orders and regulations. They did not intend to harm the woman or any of the residents. Nonetheless, the results were tragic. Later, it was reported, the woman died.

March 20th:
Memories of Bethlehem [author unknown].

Having been back in the States just a little over twenty four hours, I was awakened out of a sound sleep with a rush of adrenaline. There were flashes of light in the sky and the sound of explosions in the distance. My first thought was "Oh God they're bombing again!" It took me a few seconds, laying there in the dark, to realise I was in my own bed and the flashes of light and the sounds I had heard were only thunder and lightning. The sights and sounds of the past 3 weeks in Bethlehem will be forever etched in my memory.

Before this last trip to Bethlehem I used to see an F16 in the sky and think how incredible it must be to fly such an awesome machine. Now that I have been on their receiving end they have somehow lost their mystique. After having survived four nights of bombing by F16s in Bethlehem I now know the terror they bring. Some nights they would attack in the early evening - other nights in a predawn raid. Occasionally they would just fly overhead to tease the populace with a kind of psychological mind game. We were completely defenceless and the IAF was very much aware of that.

At the first sound of F16s flying in the distance that dreaded anticipation begins to fill your psyche. You know what is coming. Slowing, the jets begin to circle ever closer to their intended target. Then suddenly they come in fast and low screaming so loudly the sound is deafening. There is a brilliant flash of light and such a massive explosion that the ground shakes and huge buildings are reduced to rubble. The concussion shatters windows for blocks around the target and whole buildings are shaken as if mere children's toys. Then the whole process starts again and again until your nerves like the surrounding windows are shattered and sleep is impossible for the rest of the night.

Before the invasion we would walk down each morning to the target site and take pictures of the previous night's destruction. The first night they hit a small building very near my hotel in the middle of a heavily populated shopping area. It had been a small gunsmith's shop but was billed by the Israelis as a weapons manufacturing plant. The main target had been the police station and barracks in the middle of Bethlehem. It had been the only remaining Palestinian police station of any consequence left standing in the West Bank. Homes and businesses across the street and in the surrounding area were severely damaged and windows were blown out and shattered over a large area. The streets were literally covered with glass and debris. It was heartbreaking each day to see families and shopkeepers digging through the remains of their homes and businesses trying to salvage what they could. Each day I was stabbed through the heart knowing that each of these bombs and the jets that delivered such destruction were in fact paid for with my tax dollars.

Each morning life would go on seemingly as usual yet there was a general anxiety that is a consequence of life under such conditions. Most days when I would go to Beit Sahour or wherever, I knew I must be sure to be home between 4 and 5 each afternoon before the shooting started. After the bombings and shelling started it was decided I would be safer staying with Elias and his family instead of the hotel. Many afternoons I had to be dropped off in Bethlehem by friends either below Manger Square or on a street below Elias's house so that I could quickly walk or run back through the increasingly deserted streets. It was often too dangerous for cabs or friends to drive me all the way back as the road home is high and exposed in places. It was an eerie feeling to walk down the main shopping streets and find all the shops closed or closing at such an early hour. Sometimes the machine guns would have already started their sporadic firing and occasionally there were Apache helicopters hovering in the area. They frightened me as I had often watched them firing from my hotel window. Apaches are often used in targeted assassinations which many times miss their intended victim and kill innocent bystanders. One afternoon I was a little late getting back from Beit Sahour. There were helicopters circling and I ran up the steps and alleys trying to reach Elias's house as fast as possible. I had no sooner closed the door behind me when a huge explosion shook the house. Such is life under occupation.

One Monday before the invasion we set up some appointments in Jerusalem and made plans to visit the Old City. Arriving at the Bethlehem checkpoint in a hired car with yellow Israeli license plates we expected no trouble - after all we were Americans. What ensued, with absolutely no provocation on our part, was my near execution. I came within a hair of being shot and killed by an aggressive Israeli commando for absolutely no reason. If not for the intervention of another Israeli soldier I would be dead. I know I will never come as close to death as I did that day. After the incident, which left me shaking with anger and pumped full of adrenaline, we walked up to the checkpoint and demanded to speak with the officer in charge. Suddenly no one spoke English – how very convenient. Later on I did file an official protest with the American Consulate. Nothing will come of it of course but it did make me feel that I had at least done something.

During my stay in Bethlehem Ariel Sharon launched the largest and most violent incursion into the West Bank in twenty years. Beit Sahour was surrounded but was not invaded thank goodness. Beit Jala was invaded by tanks and put under curfew. Anyone caught outside his home would be summarily shot. Homes, churches and mosques were taken over by soldiers and turned into sniper outposts. Areas in Bethlehem were also invaded by tanks. For days - even in those areas free of Israeli incursions - people were afraid and shops were kept closed. There were very few cars on the streets. Hebron Road, one of the main streets of Bethlehem, was bulldozed in sections and water mains were broken and phone lines were deliberately cut. Deheisha and Aida Refugee Camps in Bethlehem were invaded under the pretence of looking for "suspected terrorists." This has become a catch-all excuse for the murder and destruction wrought on too many West Bank towns and villages. We knew of the plans to invade the refugee camps several days before it actually happened. Any terrorist hiding in the camps would have long since fled by the time the IDF invaded. Even so the Israelis arrested all the men and boys in the camps between the ages of 14 and 40. All were blindfolded and had their hands tied with plastic wire. Eventually most were released. During the invasion several innocent women and children were shot and left to bleed to death. The Israeli army refused to let ambulances and medical personnel into the camps to attend the wounded. One doctor was killed and several medical personnel were injured in attempts to help the wounded. The Red Cross was also not allowed to enter the camps.

I have never been into Aida Refugee Camp but it was closer to us and we could hear the explosions and gunfire emanating from there. During the day we could hear the wailing and shouts of the funerals. I went to Deheisha last April and know how densely populated it is. The camp covers one square kilometre and is home to 11,000 people. The tiny streets are no more than 6 to 8 feet wide and the Israelis put ten tanks inside the camp carving tunnels through what used to be people's homes. The destruction is all so senseless and so merciless. What kind of people can do such things?

After the F16 bombing raids stopped we found ourselves on the receiving end of the Israeli tanks roaming the streets of Beit Jala and those stationed across the valley in the illegal Israeli settlement of Gilo. I had been sitting by an open window one evening writing in my journal when the first missile hit. (We left the windows open to prevent them being shattered by the concussion during attacks.) I screamed and nearly jumped out of my skin as the house shook with the deafening sound of the explosion. We all ran to the stairwell of the house as it was the safest place. As the missiles continued to rain down all around us the next door neighbour called and asked us to come to his older ground floor stone house. So amid the missiles and gunfire we hurriedly ran down the back stairs in the dark to the safely of his home. Even in such times Palestinian hospitality takes over and we were offered tea and sweets. We stayed there several hours until things began to quieten down.

In the light of morning we found that the school in front of us had been hit and a home and pharmacy directly above us was hit with four missiles. Over the course of two nights it was utterly destroyed. The innocent Christian family who had been sitting in their living room during the first night's attack miraculously escaped unharmed. I could hardly choke down the tears as I walked through what had once been their lovely home. What possessions were left were covered with shards of glass and mounds of dust and debris.

The next night Bethlehem University, a Catholic institution, at the end of the street was hit. The beautiful new humanities building built by the US government was hit with four laser guided missiles. Another building near the entrance was also hit. Walking through the glass covered streets to look at the damage the next day I learned that each of these American made laser guided missiles cost $180,000. Windows were blown out all over the small campus and the cost of clean up and glass replacement alone will be substantial. Because of the sophistication of the missiles involved there is no chance these were accidents. All of these civilian targets had absolutely nothing to do with hunting suspected terrorist or the defence of Israel. This is a classic example of the wanton destruction of Palestinian infrastructure and illegal collective punishment.

I gained a new respect for the Palestinian militias this trip, who so valiantly try to defend their towns and villages. They are armed with nothing more than old rifles and some small machine guns bought on the Israeli black market. They are fighting the finest technology America can supply – F16s, Apache gunships, and tanks fitted with sophisticated laser guided missiles. They are truly freedom fighters and I gave them a smile and a thumb's up sign whenever I encountered them.

Even in the midst of all this war and destruction I never encountered even the slightest anti-American sentiment – at least not from any Palestinian. I was always treated with the utmost kindness and respect by both Christians and Muslims alike. Most Palestinians were so very grateful that we would come at such a time to try to be of help and to show our love and solidarity with them. In talking with dozens and dozens of Palestinians over the course of three weeks I never once heard anyone utter anything but an earnest desire for peace. During this trip my respect and love for the Palestinian people has grown immensely. Far from being the terrorists they are so commonly portrayed as in the American media, their courage, compassion and forgiving nature are a testimony to the finer qualities of humanity.

March 29, 2002
[Ramallah]
International civilians are trying to assist ambulance teams in Ramallah as they attempt to get to wounded and dying people. The ambulances of the International Red Cross, Red Crescent and U.N. have been prevented from moving in the city. The ambulances are now coming under fire and international civilians have been trying to act as human shields on board since 1400 today. Internationals will continue to ride aboard the ambulances in the hope that this may increase the chances of getting to those in need.

The muka'ta has been under constant tank shelling and the electricity has been cut in the city since early this morning.

Urgent from Palestine
Friends as you may be hearing, seeing or reading the situation in Palestine is desperate. Israeli forces have invaded almost every area of Ramallah and we are under heavy tank shelling and gun fire. An unidentified number of people are dead and scores are injured. Ambulances have been prevented access and soldiers are opening fire on them.

There are international civilians in the areas under fire witnessing the carnage of the Israeli soldiers wreaked on the Palestinian people. Other internationals have been beaten down for trying to get into Ramallah to help Palestinians.
Gather, march, and protest in the streets!
We need the voices of all good people around the world!
PLEASE ACT NOW

Ramallah Update

Into the evening Israeli forces continue their offensive on the Palestinian people:

- After heavy shelling of the Presidential compound all day Israeli forces entered the compound with tanks and ground troops. The Palestinian police have reported that no one has been taken but there have been office to office break-ins and searches, and resistance from the compound.
- Two Palestinian Red Crescent ambulances carrying a doctor and two foreign international volunteers - American citizen Adam Shapiro and Irish national Caoimhe Butterly - have been held up for over 3 hours, trying to reach the injured in the compound
Adam reported the ambulances being stopped and completely searched and everybody was being forced out of the ambulances.
- At the time of this writing one ambulance carrying the doctor and the two foreign civilian volunteers have been let in. One ambulance was turned back. Two injured are being removed from the compound now.
- Al-Jazeera satellite channel was showing people bleeding and lying dead on the floor of the compound as the ambulances were held at the gate, and the volunteers waiting to be let in to assist the injured could see smoke rising from the compound
- Electricity throughout Ramallah has been cut in all neighbourhoods and water tanks have been shot up, causing them to leak precious water. Israeli forces have been shooting at anything moving in the streets as their tanks are positioned throughout Palestinian neighbourhoods.
- The Shabak and Israeli police entered a hotel in Jerusalem where an international solidarity delegation of French and Swiss are staying. The Israeli forces demanded all the passports of the 50 internationals. After the intervention of embassies and lawyers the passports were returned. It is unknown whether they will attempt to forcibly remove international witnesses in the area.

- Despite this form of intimidation by the Israeli authorities and army, internationals are intent on staying and expressing their solidarity with the Palestinian people.

March 30
[Ramallah}
Two foreign civilians, U.S. citizen Adam Shapiro and Irish national, Caoimhe Butterly are stranded in Ramallah Presidential compound. The Israeli military have cut phone lines in the compound. The foreign civilians have related through text messages that the Red Cross is urgently needed in the compound. Despite the best efforts of the foreign civilians to negotiate, the Israeli army is still denying access to the Red Cross. The Israeli Defence Forces are shelling a commercial building in Ramallah with civilians trapped inside.

- 50 Foreign civilians including Americans, Canadians, Italians and French are now going to attempt to reach the Ramallah hospital to give blood and deliver medical aid. They will be moving through the streets of Ramallah, still under siege.
- American citizen Adam Shapiro is pleading for immediate international intervention to help him and the others who are trapped in the Presidential compound in Ramallah.

The Israeli military is not allowing UN ambulances into the compound to help the injured.
We have faxed American diplomat Aaron Miller and various news services including Reuters, AP, CNN, ABC, CBS and the New York Times.

Update - Ramallah
As of 15.00 today, March 30, more than 50 foreign civilians accompanied physicians and Red Crescent personnel in a civilian mission to get urgent medical aid into the presidential compound. Medics and civilians left from an area under total siege and marched past tanks deployed in the Manara. Shortly before reaching the

President's compound they were stopped and Israeli forces refused to allow them to proceed. The group protested that the Israeli military were in flagrant contravention of the Geneva Convention, as well as international humanitarian law, by choosing not to allow medical assistance to the injured. The delegation insisted that they would take medical personnel and supplies in. Finally it was agreed that two doctors, two ambulances and four foreign observers would be allowed access inside the presidential compound.

The two internationals who were inside the compound expressed their great relief to see that eventually pressure had succeeded and that medical aid was eventually allowed in. One body has been removed and the injured inside have now received medical attention.
The international delegation who accompanied the medical group comprised of Huwaida Arraf, Jose Bove a French national, and an Italian member of Parliament. They all expressed their solidarity with the Palestinians struggle for freedom and voiced their condemnation of the war policies of Sharon's government.

The foreign civilians who entered the compound went in as a symbol of the international outcry over the brutal attacks on the Palestinian people, and as a symbol of the intervention that is immediately sought from the international community. Adam Shapiro has now left the compound in exchange for one doctor and one medic. Caoimhe Butterly has remained due to her concern that medics are not being allowed free access and that her continued presence may help facilitate further assistance.

Inside the Presidential compound the foreign civilian delegation met with President Arafat. Both the President and the other Palestinians inside are in good spirits and expressed their heartfelt gratitude for the international solidarity. President Arafat stated that "Occupation is the real terrorism, and the Palestinian people will continue to struggle for their freedom. Our people will be free." The foreign delegation supported the President's statement.

March 31st
URGENT: UPDATE RAMALLAH
As of 11:30 international civilians are on scene where Israeli soldiers were storming into Palestinian homes. International civilians were demanding to see that soldiers were not harming Palestinian civilians. Soldiers verbally warned the civilians to go away and held them at gunpoint, but they stayed on the scene with a video camera. After 20 minutes the soldiers left this neighbourhood, comprised of apartment buildings full of families and children.

International civilian are now making there way towards Ramallah hospital to gather and attempt to march on the presidential compound in an effort to the stop brutal attacks going on now in Ramallah.

URGENT: IDF TRYING TO ENTER RAMALLAH HOSPITAL
Israeli APC's and tanks are in the emergency entrance of Ramallah hospital. Palestinian doctors and international civilians are blocking the entrance. The Israeli military is trying to forcibly gain access to Ramallah hospital.

Update: Ramallah
- Volunteer medic Neta Golan is riding with ambulances in the Ramallah Tahta (lower) area. She helped retrieve the two bodies that international civilians saw brought into Ramallah hospital earlier. She says that there are two more bodies that they cannot get to.
- She observed soldiers conducting house to house searches, and for people who did not open their doors they were broken down; and she saw soldiers entering, firing upon Palestinian civilians.
- Soldiers are holding Palestinian men on their knees and an Arab source (who must remain unidentified) says that the men are being divided into two groups: one group to be arrested and one group that is being summarily executed.

Update: Bethlehem
Our mayor has just announced that we expect invasion within the next hour.

12 to 15 APC's and tanks are now at the Bethlehem checkpoint with one busload of soldiers. The soldiers are not allowing press to enter at gunpoint.

Friday, April 5 2002
Some international people have been evacuated from Bethlehem. A majority of us remain. We are eighteen activists with the International Solidarity Movement, staying in the Al-Azza refugee camp in Bethlehem. We are from the UK, US, Ireland and Canada. Two of us are Jewish and one Palestinian. Electricity has just been restored and we are taking the opportunity to send out this message.

Bethlehem has been re-occupied by the Israeli armed forces and its people are under brutal siege. Everyone in the Al-Azza camp is unable to leave its perimeters to go engage in other activities that most people take for granted. There is one road that divides the camp, and we must dash across in fear of being shot at by Israeli snipers. On our first night here (just prior to the current re-occupation) our members narrowly escaped being killed as Israeli bullets whizzed past us. This is the fourth time in seventeen months that the Israeli military has re-occupied Bethlehem. They have cut the power lines like they always do. This left every home in darkness and in an information black-out, unable to find out what is happening beyond what we can see at the end of the street. All we can do is sit and listen to the sounds around us: F-16 jets, Apache helicopters, drone aircraft, tanks and armoured personnel carriers. Indeed, the entire military might of a modern army -- and we know it could be turned against this camp at any time, as it has in the past.

Even in our fear we recognise that, for us, it is only a brief and temporary experience. Those who live here have endured attacks like this time and again during the four decades of Israeli military dictatorship. Likewise, we are aware that the situation in Bethlehem may only be the beginning, if the destruction of Ramallah is any indication. At least thirty people have been executed and buried in a mass grave; Red Crescent ambulances have been fired upon and the buildings bombed. Yesterday the Israeli soldiers lifted the curfew in Ramallah, but when people left their homes to get food, seven were shot.

We also have had a two hour respite from curfew, though it could not be trusted. We tried to escort an ambulance to provide food and medical attention to the many families trapped inside the Church of the Nativity. There, in the centre of Bethlehem, the Israeli military has killed one member of the clergy, injured several others, and has now surrounded the church with around two hundred people inside. Two ambulances were crushed by a tank, and we believe the death toll in Bethlehem to be around twenty. All this has taken place within a closed military zone, with the Israeli forces having complete control over where the media are allowed to go. They have gone as far as taking shots at Arab and international press.

We see these horrors being inflicted knowing full well that our countries, especially the US, have sent the weapons and money, and provide the international backing (tacit or overt) that makes this brutality possible. Today, with the television back on, we watch demonstrations all over the world by people urging their governments to end this illegal occupation. We desperately hope they are listening, because time is running out ...
Signed,
Jake Mundy - Maia Ramnath - Liv Dillon
Phan Nguyen - Paul Stockley - Joe Gessert
Phil Boast - Jordan Flaherty
James Kirkham - Zaid Khalil
Kevin Neish - Herbert Steven Quester
John McSweeney - Kristen Schurr

Josina Manu - Martha Andrewes
Jenny McArthur - Loukas Christodoulous

March 31st
The Israeli military is holding international civilians and three
Palestinian medics in the grounds of the presidential compound. They
have been held there for over two hours. The military has requested
that the international observers leave without the Palestinian medics.
Fearing for the safety of the medical personnel the international
civilians are not leaving.

Sunday, March 31, 2002
For Immediate Release
Press Release
INTERNATIONALS IN WITH ARAFAT CALL FOR THEIR AMBASSADORS
[RAMALLAH] 50 International civilians entered Yasser Arafat's
Presidential Compound today, which is under continuous siege by the
Israeli Forces. The group of Internationals is comprised of civilian
volunteers from France, Brazil, Canada, Belgium, Britain, Ireland,
Germany, and Israel who are here on a humanitarian mission. Thirty-
four (34) international civilians remain inside. The group has stated
that they will remain inside of the Presidential Compound until the
siege is lifted; they remain in solidarity with all Palestinian people
who are now under occupation and extend their demands to include
the end of Israel's occupation of the entire West Bank and Gaza Strip.
The Israelis have cut power, phone lines and water supply to the
compound. Food is also in short supply.

The 34 foreign civilians are asking for their respective ambassadors to
urgently come to President Arafat's compound.

The city of Ramallah, where the group of internationals is currently
based, is under closure and violent occupation by Israeli Forces.
Power has been cut in most neighbourhoods of Ramallah and water

and food is in short supply in many homes, hospitals have had to resort to back-up generators and the transport of medicine and medical supplies has been disrupted. International witnesses have reported Israeli forces breaking in doors of homes and conducting mass arrests, where Palestinians have been bound and placed in torturous positions for extended periods, there have also been at least 14 extra-judicial executions performed by the Israeli Forces in the last 2 days. Medical personnel have been arrested by the Israelis and several ambulances have been confiscated. Israeli Forces also attempted to enter Ramallah Hospital earlier today but were kept out by a human blockade conducted by the Internationals.

April 2nd

0130: Ramallah. The Occupation forces are shelling a building called Jebreen Al-Rjoob. This is a government building and there are 400+ people inside, 60 of whom are women. They are prepared to fight and we fear this will be a bloodbath. Huwaida Arraf is reporting that they are still hearing constant shelling very close to where they live near the city's main hospitals.

0230: URGENT UPDATE BETHLEHEM: At the Ibda'a computer centre we are experiencing massive fighting going on outside. We can hear clearly a tank rolling by the building and there is massive tank fire, mortar fire and gun clashes. It appears that the IDF have entered Deheishe via the Ibda'a entrance. We are all on the floor as very loud shots occur outside.

0145: Five tanks are coming into Beit Sahour led by a bulldozer past the YMCA. We are experiencing helicopter fire and Deheishe refugee camp has soldiers conducting house to house searches.

Quick update:
The presidential compound in Ramallah is currently being fired upon. We still have 34 foreign peace activists inside. There is a dire shortage

of food and no water. They urgently need medical supplies. Palestinian doctors were forced to dig a mass grave in the parking lot of the Ramallah hospital today to bury 25 of the dead bodies that have been retrieved over the past 4 days. Though it is difficult to get an accurate count of the dead due to the Israeli military preventing medical workers from operating, doctors were forced to make room in the hospital morgue. We have been unable to bury the dead properly due to the Israeli siege and their open shoot policy.

A 55-year old woman by the name of Widad Majed Nimr Safwan was shot dead by Israeli snipers as she left the Ramallah hospital this morning, where she came for treatment of her broken leg. Widad left the Shiekh Khaled bin Zayed hospital at approximately 11am this morning, to have her dead body carried back by an Italian peace worker at 11:15am. Snipers shot Widad in the cheek and back of the neck.

Ramallah April 03, 2002

1230: 2,000 people including internationals, Israeli and Arab civilians in 30 buses have arrived at Aram checkpoint located just before the Qalandia checkpoint near Ramallah. Despite the horrible weather, rain, hail and wind, they have attempted to get through the siege of Ramallah to deliver humanitarian aid.

At Aram they were faced with an onslaught of tear gas so horrible that people were choking and have been made sick. Yet they are still committed to getting through and are still protesting at Aram with the demand to be allowed into Ramallah.

Israeli occupation forces have allowed one truck-load of aid out of dozens that the human rights protesters brought to go through, loaded with aid.
1255: The one aid truck the Occupation Forces allowed in, they then attacked. Soldiers took out the medical aid and stomped it into the ground. They took out sugar, flour and other food aid and dumped it

out, and threw tear gas again at the group. Earlier they shot at a UN convoy. Now they are beating the protestors with batons.
Meanwhile on the ground in Ramallah there is one ambulance still free in the city attempting to provide assistance. We have internationals on that ambulance and more international civilians are going to try to attempt to deliver bread to families who have been unable to leave their homes for food or other assistance.

Bethlehem April 03, 2002
At least 30 Palestinians injured by IDF fire continue to take shelter in the three churches of Manger Square, including the Church of the Nativity, deprived of medical supplies and food and surrounded by the IDF. Among the injuries are four critical cases. An ambulance attempting to evacuate those critically injured was crushed en route to Manger Square by an Israeli tank in Wadi Ma'ali. Those trapped in the church are desperate for medical assistance and food but are unwilling to exit the churches for fear of immediate IDF aggression. Yesterday two members of the Abda family were killed when their Bethlehem home near Manger Square was shelled. The victims, a mother in her 60s and her son, were taking shelter with the rest of their family from the IDF assault on Bethlehem. The survivors remain in the house with the bodies of their loved ones, unable to take steps for a proper burial due to the continuous IDF prescience in their neighbourhood. International civilians in the area are considering a plan to escort the Abda family to safety with their deceased, as well as to deliver medical supplies to the injured people in the Manger Square churches.

April 5th
UPDATE: WAR ON THE PALESTINIAN PEOPLE
- This afternoon, the Palestinian Red Crescent has announced the cessation of all its operations due to the ongoing and massive Israeli assaults against its hospitals, clinics, ambulances, and medical staff in all areas targeted by the current Israeli military campaign.

- In the past half hour there have been 9 male martyrs at The Church of the Nativity. This report has been confirmed by Palestinian sources from inside the church. The men were shot through the hole in the back where the door once was and through windows broken by constant gunfire.
- They have just begun firing on Balata refugee camp with American-made Apache helicopters. It is being reported that there are many casualties and deaths, but still there is no medical help available.
- In Nablus a woman died when the Occupation forces shelled her home. Her name was Zaha Sartech, age 30. - Mahmoud Alul, governor of Nablus, has had his home taken over by Occupation soldiers and it has been destroyed on the inside in typical IDF fashion.
- In the old city of Nablus the resistance is strong and, as of two hours ago, had successfully bombed 8 tanks and is keeping the Israeli military at bay around the perimeter of the old city. Unfortunately the Occupation forces have carried in explosives to many peoples homes and have destroyed them. Many people have been injured and killed but it is difficult to know how many because the ambulances cannot get in.
- In the village of Atara near Bir Zeit University a 60 year old man, named Sari, who was very ill and was trying to reach the hospital was prevented by IDF soldiers and subsequently died in the street.
- Nine international civilians left the Presidential compound today with two Red Crescent ambulances that had been permitted by the soldiers, who inspect the ambulances and decide what they will allow in, to deliver food aid but not medical aid.
- The agreement made between the Israeli army and the French consulate was that a French man suffering from a possible heart attack was to be evacuated with his wife, six other French nationals and one German woman. They were to be driven to Qalandia checkpoint between Ramallah and Jerusalem where they would be met by their respective consuls.
- There is still no word from the internationals and the ambulance drivers have not checked in.

We appeal to the world not to remain silent and to come to the Occupied Palestinian Territories to help protect the Palestinian people. WE are witnessing war crimes and must work to stop this!

April 6th

Friends,

12:30pm - A group of 25 foreign peace activists are making their way to Manger Square in Bethlehem, carrying signs highlighting sections of the Fourth Geneva Conventions and the Universal Declaration of Human Rights that are being blatantly violated by the Israeli government and military. These include the right for the wounded to receive medical attention and for pregnant women to be tended to. For over a week the Israeli army has been preventing the ambulances of the Union of Palestinian Medical Relief Committees and the Palestinian Red Crescent Society from operating, by stopping ambulances and detaining, harassing, beating and arresting medical workers. In many areas of besieged Palestine there are wounded and dead Palestinians that medical workers have been denied access to. Reports from Nablus are that many people have been buried alive under the rubble of their homes that have been destroyed by Israeli tanks and helicopter fire. The internationals are hoping that they will be able to gain access to Manger Square and the Church of the Nativity to evacuate the dead and the wounded. They are walking in front of an ambulance to provide an unarmed human shield to ambulances that have been shot at.

SOS calls from the Jenin Refugee camp! The camp, 1 km squared, home to approximately 15,000 people is being attacked by air and land. Contacts in Jenin City report heavy black smoke rising from inside the camp. Friends inside the camp are reporting heavy bombardment by tanks and helicopter gunships. Bulldozers have also been brought into the camp and are demolishing homes to make way in the narrow streets of the camp for tanks to enter.

"We have no electricity and no water. Our water tanks have been destroyed from the intensity of the Israeli bombardment. Our wives are crying and our kids are screaming. There's no television to distract them. All they are hearing is the explosions all around them. Where is the conscience of the world when we are being massacred and no one is intervening to stop it?" – Jamal Abu Al-Haije, resident of Jenin Camp.

Dr. Ali Jabareen of the Jenin Hospital reports that they need help reaching the injured and dead. People are being left to bleed in the streets and other people are being buried under the rubble of their homes. No idea how many people are dead. The hospital ambulances are not being allowed to move. UNRWA and the International Committee of the Red Cross are not able to function. Reports from Nablus are that they have also brought bulldozers into the Balata Refugee Camp.

There are random explosions throughout Ramallah. It is difficult to know what is being blown up. Innocent Palestinian civilians are being terrorised and killed. The international community has an obligation to stop this massacre. Will we wait until it's over to say that we're sorry?

Appendix 3.

Susan Barclay in Nablus: Thursday Aug 1st 2002.

Over the ensuing months, during which time I was taking a long hiatus in Latin America, the situation in the West Bank went predictably from worse, to abysmal, to well-nigh impossible. Sharon's invasions continued unabated, there was a suspected massacre at Jenin camp, in the US the Bush administration gave Israel carte blanche to continue apace with its virtual ethnic-cleansing programme and its rape of Palestinian civil society, and once again the Palestinian people found themselves under a complete lockdown in the West Bank, now divided into the long talked-of cantons. Also predictably, the suicide-bombings stepped up a notch, as Fatah, Tamzin, Hamas and Islamic Jihad's sporadic peace efforts were frustrated time and again by IDF incursions and atrocities. Leading Fatah activist and Palestinian Authority member Marwan Barghouti was kidnapped by the IDF in Ramallah during the Easter incursions, and was put on show trial in Israel in August, charged with murder and 'directing terrorism' (among other things). Gaza had long been a grim prison for its indigenous inhabitants, and now the Israeli courts began rubber-stamping the IDF's policy of expelling the families of suicide bombers and suspected militants there, alongside brutal night time house demolitions all over. The ISM, meanwhile, had organised its "Freedom Summer" campaign, and what follows is just one of the many reports that I received during this time, from Susan Barclay, a peace activist from the US.

I find a few moments to write not because it is something that I even have the time to do, but more because if I don't write now I am afraid to lose the precious, tragic stories and sights that I have witnessed in the last few weeks. During the past weeks I have lain down to sleep between two and four in the morning, to the sounds of tanks clunking over the pavement and sporadic shooting. Noises of the night that

Palestinian ears can distinguish in the flash of a moment, and a mind bursting with thoughts, scenes and stories that keep me from unconsciousness for even longer.

The morning begins with laughter as a friend tells me that he likes to watch Tom and Jerry because it makes him smile. "Why do people watch Rambo? We see that everyday—here it is not TV, it is real." When Internationals first arrive here the military machinery waging this war often baffles them, but the novelty wears off so very quickly; loss of appreciation frequently goes hand in hand with habit, routine and repetition. Today alone, I saw over fifteen tanks, seven APCs, a number of jeeps, thirty-plus soldiers armed with M16s and a Land Rover full of commandos. This is life here. Children two or three years old know the words for soldier, tank, shooting, prison, and death; slowly and surely war creeps into their beings.

The children play war frequently. One mother told me the other day, "The terribly sad thing is that they always want to be the Israelis, no one wants to be Palestinian, to be controlled, to be the victim. These little children know who has power." Another woman tells me of her discussion with a group of children about life, saying that first children talked about problems they are having—not sleeping, nightmares, constant fear—but then the conversation turned toward dreams and desires. In the midst of talk about parks, toys, and summer camp one girl raised her hand and said: "We need some milk and bread." Despite their disturbing loss of innocence, these children still manage to help me leave the mental space of many difficult realities; by playing with my hair, laughing at my Arabic, or simply sitting on my lap, they help me continually find healing, rejuvenation and great hope. The people of this land are in dire need of humanisation. As I become closer to the Palestinians living in Nablus and simultaneously start seeing the same soldiers and developing a rapport of sorts, I can't help but feel that the situation, this ongoing, long-going war is profoundly tragic. One afternoon we were attempting to get food and medical supplies to an occupied house in an area where the IDF captain has threatened us with arrest. There is an APC at the bottom of a small hill about three hundred feet from the house, where the soldiers demand that a Danish ISM volunteer and I are to stay, while Doctor Rassem and Feras Bakri go to the house to treat the child. Perhaps this is so we don't see the state of the home, or perhaps they suspect we are journalists, or perhaps it is simply about power and control—in any case, our goal is to care for the child and both Feras and the Doctor feel comfortable going without us. I watch as the ambulance heads up the hill and begin a conversation with the soldiers about "problems" in Nablus and how they feel about being here. These two young men were insistent on the fact that they want to go home, that they think over 95% of Palestinians are good, that they want peace for their children: "I just don't want my children to ride the bus in fear" Michel says. They talk about going out, dancing, not having showered in days and sleeping on the floor. They say they only shoot armed people. I ask about a recent death in Balata refugee camp, when a twenty-four year-old was shot in the head by soldiers in a jeep. Maybe he had a gun they say; maybe rocks, I reply.

They share hopes for the future and claim that there is a violent cycle that is incessantly repeating itself here - suicide bombing, invasion, bombing, invasion. I ask how they think they are helping end the problems and they say, "By being here—no bombings in twenty-plus days." "And when you leave?" I ask. "Or do you plan to stay forever?" They seem completely ignorant of their role in creating further bombings, blind to the fact that they are only rendering a population more desperate, more hopeless, and more deprived each and every day, pushing people towards the "nothing to lose" state that a suicide bomber has invariably reached. And then it is time to change shifts and three new soldiers pull up in an APC and these two men, Michel and Avi, climb into the new APC and head into town to do I-can-imagine-what. These interactions put faces to these monstrous military machines; I think of the APCs that only a few hours earlier terrorised an adjacent neighbourhood; during house searches soldiers took one man and beat him for over thirty minutes. I saw him this morning and now I see Michel and Avi beating any one of my Palestinian friends, and I am left in total confusion. These are just young men beating, shooting, and terrorising other young men because they see the enemy. Seeing humanity makes the destruction of life seems so senseless, so unbelievable. I think that is part of our work here, each one a tiny thread weaving humanity into hearts, souls, minds, and moments and trying to shelter the remaining flickers of hope from the wild wind of war.

One of my dearest friends Khowla was walking by my side the other night, discussing dreams and talking about her youth. "When I was young I had so, so many dreams. I wanted to be a lawyer, to study biology, to go to university, travel, and learn about everything. But Susan, when you see the situation go from bad to worse again and again and again, all your dreams get broken." She is only twenty-one. There is still so much time, I say as I squeeze her hand. The director of the Ministry of Education, Juman Karaman, welcomed us into her home a few days ago; she lives in a home adjacent to one that is occupied, where we were headed. She explained how very far behind the students were due to constant closures and called this second term "a complete catastrophe". Final exams were scheduled for June 17th - July 4th, but Nablus was invaded on June 20th; exams were put on hold and students have been in the state of exam preparation ever since. When curfew is lifted for a few hours, which has happened for a total of thirty hours in the forty-two days of the current curfew - in Israeli prisons the detainees are given more than an hour per day recreation - students rush to the school and take an exam. They are currently waiting for another curfew lift, to finish their exams, studying now for over a month, and never knowing on what day they will have to perform. Juman believes that education is not really about how much time students spend studying, but rather about quality. With the constant closures and the closing of surrounding villages, teachers were habitually confronting tanks, APCs, and soldiers en route to their schools. She asked us to imagine the state of a teacher who finally arrives at school, after having journeyed between one and three hours in constant fear, wading through life-threatening circumstances; "How well can this person teach?" As for the students, she added: "After hours of shooting, nerves worn very thin, constant uncertainty and fear, how can they possibly learn?"

After more than a month imprisoned in their homes people are restless, frustrated, lethargic, angry, humiliated, and saturated. They are using the small amount of money they had, unable to make anymore, and the financial situation is increasingly dire. I was having tea yesterday with a man who mutters: "Maybe I can carry ten kilos, twenty, or fifty, but eventually I will break. Everyone has a limit." We are in an occupied house and talking to the man now living in the basement with thirty or so soldiers on the top three floors. These thirty-plus soldiers mean five APCs are parked out front, mesh covers the windows like giant spider webs, and the night reverberates with incessant shooting and loud music—the family has not slept well in over twenty-five days. The soldiers ask his children how they are, and the children say "not good." The father says to me, "I want to tell my children about peace, but how can I when we are living like this? They don't believe it."

During the last week, the city of Nablus had been rather quiet during the day and many people had been breaking curfew, coming out of their homes to open a shop or buy a few things. The night is still plagued by military operations, the sounds of tanks, gunfire, and surreptitious movement. The villages have been the focal point of the military during the past days, as they claim to be hunting the "terrorists" responsible for this or that suicide bombing or settlement incident. "They use the same stories again and again, killing the same terrorists three, four or five times," the local press told me a few nights ago. The villages lie to the Southwest of Nablus, little clumps of homes nestled in olive groves and rolling hills, accessible only by thin dirt roads. This week, they spent three days going village to village looking for anywhere between three and eight men. They killed three men the first day and denied the ambulance access to the bodies. A group of us went out to Sara village and attempted to get the ambulance in just to take the bodies, but they told us we had to wait until they had finished their operation. Our refusal to leave was met with physical force: kicking, hitting and shoving twenty non-violent activists come to simply take the dead.

The next morning I went with the ambulance to get the bodies, as the Israeli army had finally given their okay. We wandered up a hill to an olive grove and found a very large group of men there, who were being searched and sorted into two groups. They had come to see the bodies and help, and ended up being subject to search and arrest. They were separated into two groups, those aged 15-50 (over seventy-five men) and the very young and very old (over forty-five people). IDs were taken and the men all sat on the ground waiting as about twenty soldiers milled about and the paramedics waited for the final okay to head up the one-hundred metres to the bodies. As we watch this process, counting the men and asking the soldiers questions, we see another group of over sixty men being led down the hill towards the paved road. We are finally allowed to go get the bodies and as the medical team moves up the hill, the men who have been sitting down get up and follow en masse. We all arrive at three mounds covered by off-white tarpaulins that are removed by the paramedics. People crowd in to see who the dead are, and chaos reigns as people move from one corpse to the next.

One man has a large hole in his head and his brain is literally oozing out of his head. The second has no leg from the knee down and several large bullet wounds in his chest and groin. A third has an enormous hole in what was his forehead, and we all see that his brain is completely missing. No one knows the men, thus they think they must be workers who pass through the villages to avoid the checkpoints and soldiers; they are certainly not terrorists. I ride in the ambulance to the morgue at Rafidia hospital, sitting in the back next to the bodies, overcome by the smell, by death. We return to the Union of Palestinian Medical Relief (UPMRC) centre where I sit for a moment, trying to catch my breath and find a few words; awoken from my sombre silence by a call to tell me that soldiers have left Sara and are now in Tel. We have to move.

During this time, three Internationals have gone with the men, the sixty or so, who were rounded up and kept on the paved road. They had been led through the hills and back roads two by two, all their IDs taken and eventually large trucks come, handcuff the men and take them to a local military base. The three ask to be arrested with them, but the soldiers don't want any Internationals today. They return to Sara village on foot and while talking with locals hours later, hear cheering and find that the large majority of these men have come back. The leave to meet us in Tel, a village a kilometre from Sara. Tel is in the same situation—foot soldiers wandering in the fields, snipers on the hills, tanks, APCs and jeeps patrolling. I ask a soldier at a tank "What are you doing today?" "There are three terrorists free." "But you killed three men yesterday…" "There are many."

We continue down the road towards Tel and come across an APC, two large trucks, and soldiers forcing handcuffed Palestinians inside. This is the Tel round up…. taking all of the local men for interrogation. We walk towards them, but they are leaving, and so we deal with what they have left behind: nine donkeys, dozens of jars of traditional yoghurt, and scattered possessions. We set off with the donkeys and belongings towards Tel to meet the other Internationals and the medical team that has gone to deliver vaccinations. The military operation in Tel seems to be coming to a close; the jeeps and APCs have left and so we return to Nablus, leaving a few behind to sleep in the village. The next morning, we get news from the next village, Iraq Boreen, one kilometre from Tel and two from Sara. The IDF is still looking for their terrorists and has rounded up all the local men at a school/women's centre in town. There are already Internationals in the village and those of us in Nablus head off to the village. We begin the long walk along the small dirt path towards the village, and we see dozens and dozens of soldiers wandering through the olive groves below the village that sits on a breathtaking butte. We are denied entry into the village by soldiers at a junction and told to wait. We do wait, just until a bus arrives for some soldiers; we use this distraction as a chance to walk right past them, despite their echoing "Stop, stop."

In the village we find that the large majority of the men have been released but the remaining men cannot get their IDs back. It is clear that one of the three jeeps is ready to leave with their IDs so volunteers sit on the ground to block its path. We are able to thwart the jeep movements for a while and create quite a scene, which the Palestinians support, saying that whether we go or stay they will have problems, so we might as well stay. The jeep and soldiers eventually manages to remove enough Internationals to pull forth; they return the IDs to the men and leave us talking to the Palestinians. We split in two, some staying the village, some walking back into Nablus. We have been doing a lot of roadblock removals during the last few days. The Israeli army has closed every single village repeatedly and the Internationals staying in Iraq Boreen heeded the locals' call to remove these roadblocks. A group of nearly forty of us headed out to Tel, Iraq Boreen and New Nablus and removed three roadblocks one morning. It was incredibly beautiful to watch this simple success - working for a few hours and then watching as water trucks, vegetables and taxis begin to pass - encouraged by the sound of our clapping and the smiles of resistance. Palestinians at the Iraq Boreen roadblock then asked us to come to Salem village, where we helped remove three other roadblocks. We left a few people in the village who called an hour or two later to say that an APC and tank had come and a bulldozer was reported to be on its way. We moved quickly and had Internationals there in time to block the bulldozer. Five people sat on the ground and the bulldozer was unable to re-do the roadblock; the jeeps, however, did come and the soldiers began threatening arrest. After thirty minutes they began taking the men, one by one, quickly cuffing each one with plastic handcuffs and blindfolding them. They were put in the back of an APC and taken to Huwara military base, then released hours later after refusing to say anything. We stayed in the area until they left, knowing that they would bulldoze during the night. The day after we came again to remove the roadblock, and will continue this resistance for so long as the Palestinians want us to do so.

The quiet has been replaced with the familiar sound of tanks, jeeps and shooting again. The bombing yesterday at the Hebrew University in Jerusalem has led to a greater military presence and four or five people were injured today from tank machine-gun fire, one of them this morning right in front of my eyes in Balata refugee camp. What are they doing? One might think the Israeli army targets certain people, or roams the city with a military aim. The reality is that a very large part of their work is about terror. This morning in Balata, they came in jeeps and began tear-gassing everyone in sight for over an hour. Balata is one of the only places in Nablus that actively resists the Israeli army and succeeds - the children and young boys throw stones and impede the tanks from entering into the camp regularly. Our role this morning was not to negotiate or approach the tanks but rather to be witnesses, and attempt to discourage shooting by putting our bodies on the line.

Two tanks are sitting in an open field at the southern entrance of the camp; the children and boys are fifty metres from them with us. We make ourselves visible and watch as the children and boys throw stones and push the tanks back. The tanks play cat and mouse for over two hours with the youth, racing forward and shooting into the air, rushing the crowd and letting out huge smoke clouds, then pulling back as the children race back out to throw more stones. After over two hours of this we retreat back three or four metres to some shade and sit as most the Palestinians mill about, seeming tired of these games. All of a sudden there is tank machine-gun fire directly overhead us and shrapnel hits a seventeen year-old boy in the head. I turn and see blood pouring down this young man's face, a metre in front of me. Everyone runs with him to a nearby clinic and the Internationals watch them go and turn towards the tanks that are beginning to retreat. What kind of military operation is this? All day they have been wandering the streets, firing at will and terrorising. Things are closed again despite the fact that today marks the fourteenth day straight without any lifting of the curfew - two weeks without even an hour to go outside. Israeli - American-made - F-16s bombed Gaza and we watched Al-Jazeera news, as the numbers of those dead and injured rose ever higher, reaching over 170 (with 155 injured and fifteen killed) by 2:30am, when the news broadcast ended. I sat with seven young Palestinian men at the UPMRC centre watching the people shift through the rubble looking for more and more bodies, followed by flashes of the hospital in total chaos. Horribly, graphic images flashed across the TV screen, particularly those of children no longer recognisable as human, but I was most touched by the young man next to me, as I watched one tear roll down his cheek, and felt that I too was going to cry. Israel had agreed to pull out of the cities in the West Bank as part of recent negotiations, and Hamas and Islamic Jihad had just called for an end to suicide bombings that night. Midnight rolls around and Israeli forces bomb an apartment building without any prior warning and with complete and total disregard for the lives inside, with the very intention of destroying them. The morning after, Hamas, Fatah, PLFP, and Islamic Jihad state loud and clear: Israel is not yet ready for peace, Israel does not want peace. Suicide bombings are sure to follow. Can the world not see that Israel does not want peace? I can only imagine how this horrific incident is being spun in the US. Incessant stories about a Hamas member, with little to no mention of the entire building of civilians. I bet that no-one in the US saw the mangled children being shelved away at the hospital morgue, the father who went mad as he watched his son die on the hospital bed, the young boy with a severely charred leg. Or the mother lying covered in blood, an oxygen mask over her face and her child on her lap. What kind of a war is this? "They are trying to make life as unbearable as possible," a friend told me yesterday, "economically, medically, psychologically, and physically." That night we saw the creation of hell on earth - hatred, evil, fear, and terror. "Where is the peace?" somebody says; but everyone is silent.

This adorable seventy year-old man from a nearby village greeted me the morning after. He asked me only: "Did you see the children?" referring to Gaza. I say, "Yes" and watch as tears well up in his eyes and continue speaking for him. Imagine everything that he has seen in this lifetime and yet still, the loss of life, the death of innocent people, the killing of children makes these small streams of salt-water flow from his soul.

Notes and References

Introduction.

[i] 'Lonely Planet: Israel & the Palestinian territories', Lonely Planet, 1998.

[ii] Herzl was the highly successful reviver of the ancient version of the Hebrew language, which had already fallen out of common usage 300 years before the birth of Christ.

[iii] The Prime Minister of Israel prior to Ariel Sharon, from 1999-2000, Barak oversaw much of the dividing up of the West Bank into apartheid-style bantustans via the consolidation of modern settler-only highways. Major General Barak was formerly head of the IDF planning branch, and served as Deputy Commander of the Israeli force in Lebanon. He was also Head of the Intelligence Branch at the IDF General Headquarters. In 1986 he was appointed Commander of the IDF Central Command, and in 1987 Deputy Chief-of-Staff. In 1991 he assumed the post of Lt. General, the highest in the Israeli military. He is also notorious for having disguised himself as a woman to sneak into Lebanon and 'take out' a member of the Black September gang, who assassinated part of the Israeli team during the Munich 1973 Olympics.

[iv] I am aware that some Palestinians may take exception to this term, as it refers to Palestine purely in relation to the Hashemite Kindom of Jordan; I use it here merely for the sake of convenience, and I apologise unreservedly for any offence given.

[v] The pre-1967 borders of the state of Israel.

[vi] The London & Manchester Guardian, p.13, August 14th 2001.

[vii] In the week that I spent there, our 'delegation' was almost entirely 50-50 British/American.

Getting there.

[viii] Tel Aviv international airport.

[ix] The International Solidarity Movement.

[x] Non-Violent Direct Action.

xi I have an Egyptian stamp on my passport.

xii The Israeli Defence Forces, the official army of Israel. Most Israeli men and women have to do a period of conscripted service whilst in their youth: some religious students and, for obvious reasons, Arab-Israelis are exempt, although not Druze-Israelis. Men must do three years, and women two. The IDF is descended from the Haganah and the Irgun ('the organisation') who helped to drive the Palestinian refugees of the 1948 war from their villages and towns.
"Surveys also suggest that 40% of job advertisements stipulate 'army service necessary', thereby excluding Israeli Arabs." *PSC factsheet: 'Palestine – the New Apartheid.'*

xiii The Palestine Centre for Rapprochement. PCR is a community service center with a global vision. "Serving the local Palestinian community through the hardships of occupation policies, it shares in developing the community's physical and human resources and activating youth in their community service and development. It has a genuine commitment, and a history of working for peace. Dialogues aimed at developing mutual understanding, activating participants to work for peace and justice, educating and training for peace and reconciliation, and the work to increase the public role in building a just and lasting peace in the region, are high on the agenda of priorities of PCR. Activating people in non-violent resistance against the occupation and for human and national rights is a long-standing commitment for PCR, together with advocating peace and justice, both locally and internationally. PCR believes in community-based work. 70% of the human resources needed in any project should be provided through voluntary work provided by the community. To sustain a high level of independence in defining needed projects and in order not to become a fund oriented organization, PCR intends to preserve the tradition of minimizing its running cost and increase dependence on communal voluntary work." *Source: www.rapprochement.org*

xiv A shared taxi, basically a small minibus.

Settle down…

xv Allegra Pacheco, *'The new Intifada: resisting Israel's apartheid'*, ed. Roane Carey, p.187. Verso 2001.

xvi For a full account of this incident, go to www.adot.com/women.

xvii Liz, who you might remember from chapter one blanked me at Tel Aviv international airport to facilitate my smooth entry into Israel, is a 48-year old social worker from Stamford Hill in North London with two grown-up children. Hanna, on the other hand, is a 74-year old grandmother and a veteran of the Haganah, who fought for Israeli independence and statehood in the 1948 war. Jewish and born in Germany, her parents had brought her to Palestine as a young girl in the 1930s to escape the nazis: the rest of her family perished in the concentration camps. Realising little by little that many of her senior officers in the Haganah and those leading the Zionist terrorist outfits the Irgun and the Stern gang were the same people, she had - over the years - come to a gradual realisation of the racist oppression that the state of Israel had come to represent. She came to Britain in 1958 when her husband at the time took up a post at Bristol university, and as this process of re-evaluation continued, Hanna went from Zionist to non-Zionist to anti-Zionist. She finally renounced her Israeli citizenship in 1992. She had addressed a meeting of the Palestine Solidarity Campaign, of which she is a member, just before we had come out in December, detailing her wealth of experience. She told the meeting that 'Lenin had a term for people who will do whatever you tell them when you want them to. He called them useful idiots, and that is what we were.'

xviii 'As an occupier, the Israeli government has no sovereign claims to the water resources in the territories. And yet, since 1967 Israel has plundered and pillaged over 80% of those resources. Israel's water company, Mekoroth, has drilled thirty-two wells in the occupied territories. These wells not only serve the Jewish settlements; they have become "the principal reservoir of drinking water for Tel Aviv, Jerusalem and Beer Sheva and the most important long-term source in the [national] water system." The Palestinians, on the other hand, are required [under the Oslo accords] to pay the Israelis for any water obtained from the Israeli water company.' Allegra Pachecho, from *THE*

NEW INTIFADA: resisting Israel's apartheid', ed. Roane Carey, p.196, Verso 2001.

xix 'As part of the Oslo 2 negotiations, the Israeli government proposed that it pave several roads to facilitate the IDF's redeployment. According to numerous reports – which have never been reputed by PA officials – the Palestinian Authority agreed without conducting a thorough investigation of the maps of the road plan. The plan actually involved full-scale construction of a 400-kilometre alternative highway system for settlers, *parts of which the Israeli government had prepared years before* [my emphasis]. Until the Oslo process, the Israeli government never had the pretext of Palestinian consent to confiscate the huge amounts of Palestinian land needed to pave these roads. The PLO signature to Oslo 2 gave the Israelis just what they needed…Israel began uprooting and levelling approximately 5,000 dunams of one of the best Palestinian grape vineyards in the West Bank, destroying a centuries-old industry in the Halhoul area.' Allegra Pachecho, p.192, *ibid.*

xx Rubber bullets.

xxi "The tons of tear gas and pepper spray munitions Seattle police used on demonstrators and bystanders alike at the anti-WTO demonstrations last December contained chemicals implicated in lung problems, eye damage and even death. According to manufacturers' documents, military research and medical literature, each of these agents carries short and long-term health risks; various formulations contain potential carcinogens. Tear gas and pepper spray cause health problems even when used within guidelines on healthy people." *From "Tear Gas And Pepper Spray Can Be Deadly", In These Times, Terry J. Allen, 2000. Terry J. Allen can be reached at tallen@igc.org.*

xxii "It was like a war zone," says Russell Sparks, a student from Bellingham, Washington, who helped block a Seattle intersection on December 1. "The police rolled up in humvees, and I heard the clink, clink of cops jogging toward us. Within seconds the area was filled with gas and the air was pure white all around. I coughed and coughed. I felt like I was on fire, my friend and I both became hysterical. He fell down. A middle-aged man near me passed out, eyes open, shaking, dry heaving, twitching in the shoulders. A woman passed out face down. I tried to

help but my eyes were burning and I was screaming for medical help."
Ibid.

xxiii "While tear gas and pepper spray are banned from use in war by an international treaty, domestic use is legal and nearly ubiquitous in the United States. The advantages of these "non-lethal" technologies, police say, include fewer deaths and serious injuries to officers and suspects, a more benign image for departments and less litigation. Currently, more than 90 percent of the country's police departments issue pepper spray to their officers, according to the Justice Department, and many departments store tear gas for use in crowd control or riot situations. Despite widespread use, none of the agents sold for police purposes is monitored, tested or regulated by any government agency for consistency, purity, toxicity or even efficacy." *Ibid.*

xxiv Christian Peacemaker Team.

xxv *'Lonely Planet: Israel & the Palestinian territories', Lonely Planet Publications, September 1999.*

xxvi 'The dispute has its origins in Abraham …who made a covenant with God (Genesis 17) and also purchased the Cave of Machpelah from Ephron the Hittite (Genesis 23) as a burial place for his wife Sarah. When Abraham died, his sons Ishmael and Isaac buried him beside [her]. Later, Isaac and his wife Rebecca and Jacob and his wife Leah were all also entombed in the cave (Genesis 49: 29-32, 50:7-9, 12-14). The site became sacred to Jews and, following the 7th century sweep of Islamicism, to Muslims also…today's Ibrahimi mosque was built over the cave.' *Ibid.*

xxvii Beit Sahour is about 80% Christian.

xxviii If you're really interested in this sort of thing, then read Amira Hass's *'Drinking the sea at Gaza', Owl books, 1996.* Although it refers specifically to the Gaza strip, the comparisons are obvious. The only time that I found a satisfactorily speedy internet connection was in Bir Zeit, a university town close to Ramallah.

xxix This was so that I wouldn't have to carry hard-copy notes back through Israeli security at Ben-Gurion airport, and thus face further harassment.

xxx Again, for more on this, see *'Drinking the sea at Gaza', Amira Hass, Owl books, 1996.*

Ramallah.

xxxi Western European Jews.

xxxii For more on this, see *'The Thirteenth Tribe', Arthur Koestler, Random House 1976.*

xxxiii By which of course I mean 'entity'. The modern nation state has only been in existence for a couple of hundred years, and there is no reason to suppose that it might last that much longer.

xxxiv In AD70. 'The insistence of the mad emperor Caligula that his image be installed in the Temple was a catalyst for extremist elements to whip up the more moderate Jews into a countrywide open revolt in 66AD (the first revolt). It took four years for the Romans to quell the uprising; and it was only after a prolonged siege that in 70AD the Roman general Titus breached the walls of Jerusalem. In retaliation for this, the temple was completely destroyed and the Jews were sold into slavery or exiled abroad.' *'Lonely Planet: Israel & the Palestinian Territories', Lonely Planet, 1999.*

xxxv The timing of such arbitrary reprieves is often not announced until ten minutes or so before the event; although, just as often, such a neighbourhood might not be allowed limited freedom of movement for several days, or even as much as a week.

xxxvi Palestine Solidarity Campaign.

xxxvii In west Beirut, south Lebanon, partly the scene of the notorious 'Sabra and Shatila' massacre in 1982, for which Israeli Prime Minister Ariel Sharon – who was Israeli Defence Minister at the time – is currently facing war crimes proceedings in Belgium.

xxxviii The dominant party within the Palestinian Authority.

xxxix The Islamic Resistance Movement, a popular fundamentalist party.

xl "We shall use the ultimate force until the Palestinians come crawling to us all fours… When we have settled the land, all the Arabs will be able to do will be to scurry around like drugged roaches in a bottle." *Israeli Chief of Staff Rafael Eitan, New York Times, 14th April 1983.*

"One million Arabs are not worth a single Jewish fingernail." *Rabbi Ya'acov Perin in his eulogy at the funeral of mass murderer Baruch Goldstein, New York times, 28th February 1994.*

The Media War.

[xli] With particular regard to this, see the excellent *Four arguments for the abolition of television,* Jerry Mander, Quill, 1978.

[xlii] It is a widely acknowledged fact that IDF army checkpoints do not deter suicide bombers, as is incessantly claimed by the Israeli authorities and their apologists, and that their true purpose is to humiliate and degrade the Palestinian people. Such is the ubiquity of these checkpoints in the occupied territories that if this were really the case, then there would be no suicide bombings inside of the Green Line. Suicide bombers are generally fit young men who can easily make their way across hillsides and rough terrain and around such obstacles. In fact, it can quite reasonably be argued that paramilitary activities only serve the long-term interests of the Zionist State. In many obtainable internal memoranda from the past 50 years, it has been stated over and again that Israel wants to annex the West Bank and Gaza, but for demographic reasons this is currently impracticable. What it would therefore prefer would be an all-out war that it would win, thus enabling it to expel the Palestinian population without an international fuss. For an in-depth report on this, see *'Imperial Israel and the Palestinians'*, Nur Masahla, Pluto Press, 2000.

[xliii] For more on this, see *'Pirates and Emperors'*, Noam Chomsky, Black Rose books, 1991.

Salfit.

[xliv] This incident is referred to in slightly more detail in the 'settle down…' chapter.

Nablus.

[xlv] It should be noted that for these purposes, the term 'martyr' refers to Palestinians murdered indiscriminately by the occupation forces and not, for example, to suicide bombers.

[xlvi] The 'Nakba', or 'catastrophe', is how a great many Palestinians refer to the declaration of the state of Israel in 1948.

[xlvii] On March 14th 2002, the news section of yahoo.com reported that on the previous day, IDF troops had taken over the building that houses Associated Press during their siege of Ramallah. This was presumably so that they could engage Palestinian militants in combat without the added danger of their coming under return fire.

[xlviii] The other hotel, the Paradise - also in Bethlehem – was shelled and then used to position snipers by the IDF, during an invasion of the adjacent Al-Azza refugee camp in early December 2001, and after the ISM had used it for accommodation during their initial campaign of civil disobedience the previous August.